HOW TO WIN A PULLET SURPRISE

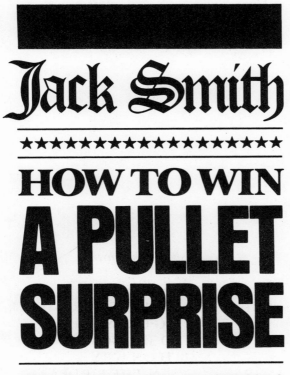

Jack Smith

****

HOW TO WIN A PULLET SURPRISE

THE PLEASURES AND PITFALLS ★★★ OF OUR LANGUAGE ★★★

A GROLIER COMPANY

FRANKLIN WATTS
New York / Toronto
1982

Grateful acknowledgment is made for the use of excerpted material from the following works, reprinted by permission:

Mrs. Byrne's Dictionary of Unusual, Obscure, and Preposterous Words by Josefa Heifetz (University Books, Inc.) copyright © 1974 by Josefa Heifetz; *Holes in a Stained Glass Window* by Norman Corwin (Lyle Stuart Inc.) copyright © 1978 by Norman Corwin; *Pullet Surprises* by Amsel Greene (Scott, Foresman and Company) copyright © 1969 by Scott, Foresman and Company.

Library of Congress Cataloging in Publication Data

Smith, Jack Clifford, 1916-
How to win a Pullet Surprise.

Selections from the author's column in the Los Angeles Times
1. English language—Style.   I. Title.
PE1421.S58   1982   808'.042   82-11142
ISBN 0-531-09874-5

Printed in the United States of America

To Cris, Adriana, Alison and Casey,
who will inherit our wonderful language.

*"In 1957, Eugene O'Neill
won a Pullet Surprise."*

from an essay by a pupil
in Miss Amsel Greene's
high school composition class

FOREWORD

This is a book about some of the delights and perils of writing and speaking English, which Ogden Nash, with irreverent affection, once called "our wonderful orangutanguage."

It is neither pedagogical nor authoritative; I am not a scholar, grammarian or philologist, or any other kind of expert. I am merely an English-speaking American who has managed to escape hard labor most of his life by writing for a living and who also, in forty years of marriage, has managed to adapt English to the needs of that sometimes exasperating institution, which has a language of its own.

This is not a comprehensive guide to contemporary usage, nor a catalogue of right and wrong. But I abhor vandalism, gobbledygook and pretentiousness in our language as much as Edwin Newman, John Simon, William Safire and Tom Middleton do; and for instruction in these matters I commend the reader to their excellent books.

My hope is that the reader who loves and enjoys the language, and is sometimes frustrated by it, will find my adventures and misadventures in it amusing if not exemplary, and may be reminded of his own.

This book was not written by a committee; it is one man's opinion, and any errors or solecisms in it, except those specifically ascribed to other sinners, are mine.

But it would not have reached print without the help of Curtis Kelly, Arthur Pine, Marilyn Kelker and of course my wife, Denise, who "processed" most of it on our brand new home computer while I was whimpering under the covers with pneumonia.

I want especially to thank my Greek chorus—the readers and correspondents whose participation gives this book its other voice, and proves that our language is alive.

J.S.

CONTENTS

HOW TO WIN A PULLET SURPRISE

THE PERILS OF SYNTAX

A cat with a broom in his underwear?

As anyone knows who has ever written so much as a letter home to mother, the English language is full of traps and pitfalls. It is harder to write a clear sentence than to keep a clear conscience.

No matter how carefully one puts his words together, he is always in danger of being misunderstood by some reader for whom they have a slightly different meaning, for whom his imagery produces slightly different visions.

Some time ago, while trying to explain why I thought my neighborhood had that elusive quality known as ambience, I wrote this sentence, describing an incident that had occurred on my front porch:

"A man chasing a cat with a broom in his underwear is ambience by any definition."

Oddly enough, several people evidently misunderstood that simple sentence. I was vexed. Any writer is vexed when he writes what seems to him as clear a sentence as the language permits, only to have literate and intelligent readers find it ambiguous or, worse, infer something quite the opposite of his meaning.

"It was with considerable interest," wrote Bob Byrne, "knowing that you also have long suffered with a back problem, that I read that you keep a broom in your underwear. Is this good?"

The problem seems to be that the reader's understanding is colored or distorted by his own experience and imagination.

"A gray tomcat with a broom in his underwear is ambience," wrote Mrs. Cecil T. Brown of Sun City, "in anyone's language. Please call us collect the next time. We will take pictures."

Another reader, Eileen Whiting of Los Angeles, also thought there were picture possibilities. "I hasten to tell you," she wrote, "that if you ever again run into that cat with a broom in his underwear—grab your camera. The picture should make Page 1."

"I do agree," wrote yet another, Mrs. Louis A. Reed of Canoga Park, "Mt. Washington must have ambience—a cat in underwear, indeed! And even more ambient—a cat with a *broom* in his underwear? But the man chasing the cat with a broom in his underwear must have a surplus of ambience or he would fall down laughing at such a sight. A Cary Grant type, I suppose."

"I have known cats for many years," wrote N. S. Elliott of Hollywood, "but have never seen one wearing underwear. Or outer wear, either, for that matter. Or was it you with the broom in your underwear? If so, why? Were you in the process of making a cup of coffee, dusting the furniture, and sweeping the floor when you first noticed the cat? I am very much interested in this. Please advise."

"I am completely confused about a portion of your column," wrote Mrs. S. A. Joseph of Ventura. "You mention 'a cat with a broom in his underwear.' Would he not be more uncomfortable than ambient? Or did you mean the *man* was? I would appreciate a clarification."

What I would like to do now is to explain exactly what happened that night, so there will be no misunderstanding.

We had a new tomcat in the neighborhood, and he had begun to exasperate me beyond the limits of my patience, if not my sanity. He would wait until I had gone to bed, or was about to, then skulk into our yard and crouch in the ivy under my window to caterwaul his loathsome lovesong.

Among all my virtues, I like to think that a tolerance for my fellow creatures is first. But the screech of a prurient tomcat strings me out. So that night, when he did it again, I snapped. My reaction was purely an atavistic reflex. I won't go into the ludicrous details.

But if you had been there, you would have seen a man chasing a cat with a broom in his underwear.

As you see, the difficulty of saying exactly what you mean, so that your reader can't fail to understand, is not a common skill, which is why most writing is not so much read as puzzled out. By rearranging the syntax, filling in the ellipses and faking out the ambiguities, we arrive at what might be called a fair working interpretation of the message.

Simple exposition being that difficult, I am not surprised, though nonetheless dismayed, to hear that an account I gave of a recent trip to our home down in Baja California was not universally understood concerning the question of whether or not my friend Gomez's parrot is still alive. I would be much happier if I could simply forget it, but the story seems to have caused so much uncertainty and disputation that I suppose I am obliged to clarify the facts.

I had driven down to the house alone one weekend to paint our iron window grilles and, as usual, stopped in at Gomez's little store to say hello and make my presence on the landscape known. There is more chance that God will put water in our pipes if Gomez knows we're there.

Gomez showed me his new parrot, which he was keeping in a cage outside the window of the kitchen in back of the store, and told me he had been trying to teach it to talk, to no avail. It was apparent that Mrs. Gomez did not like the bird, which squawked unpleasantly every time Gomez appeared, and Gomez himself had become disenchanted because of its failure to talk.

"Someday," he told me, "if he does not talk, I will cook him."

It was that remark, evidently, that led to the confusion. Instantly it made me think of the old Yiddish joke told by Leo Rosten, in which two young men give their thrifty old mother a talking parrot for company, and when they ask her later how she liked him, she says, "He was delicious."

Gomez had invited me to come back Sunday evening for dinner. Mrs. Gomez has few peers in the preparation of Mexican dishes, and I eagerly accepted. But when I sat down at her table, Gomez's remark and the Rosten story came back to mind. I will take the liberty of repeating, as I remember it, the passage in my earlier account of this affair that seems to be the crux of the question.

"The main dish was what appeared to be a small chicken, stewed in onion sauce. She served me a rather dainty leg. Suddenly it occurred to me that I hadn't heard a peep from Gomez's parrot. My fork stopped in midair.

" 'How is your parrot?' I asked Gomez.

" 'He is fine,' said Gomez. 'How is your chicken?'

"I took a bite of succulent leg. 'He is delicious,' I said sincerely."

Of the inquiries I have received, the one from Emily H. Daniels of North Hollywood seems the most urgent.

"The fate of Gomez's parrot," she writes, "has become the subject of hot debate in our household. Friends, visiting relatives and all those who cross our threshold are forced to take a stand on the vital issue of whether the parrot was eaten or not. So far our guests have unanimously agreed that the bird was consumed, but my husband Marc, the TV director, insists that the parrot is still sitting contentedly in his cage.... Marc argues that Gomez's wife never would have dared to cook the parrot, and even if she had, a man of your discernment never would have eaten it.

"Ever since your column appeared Marc has been carrying the clipping around in his pocket. At all our dinner parties he has demanded that everyone read it and then take a stand. Many of our pleasant little gatherings have turned raucous and violent as a result.

"By my somewhat unreliable count, to date, seventy-six people have voted that you ate the parrot (or at least a leg), while one has voted that you did not. I would appreciate it if you would give us the true facts."

Alas, the truth is, I'm afraid, that I can't give her an answer one way or another, as an absolute fact. Only Mrs. Gomez knows for sure, I suppose, and I certainly can't ask her.

One simply doesn't ask a lady if her chicken was a parrot.

LARKS AND SALMONS

Why don't they call mongooses mongeese?

"Have you any explanation," writes Emily Weldon of Oceanside, "as to why we don't pluralize the names of some fish? We say, 'I caught some salmon, four trout and one hundred sardines.' That's always interested me."

The truth is, I have consulted all my standard authorities on questions of usage and all I know as a result is that trouts and salmons are also correct as plurals, but people rarely use them.

I have received some correspondence on the subject, most of it entertaining but unenlightening, like the couplet sent by Syble Lagerquist, a neighbor of mine:

> *One trout, two trout, three trout, or four;*
> *Salmon are singular—twenty or more.*

I also have a scholarly two-page typewritten letter on the subject from a man in Claremont who wishes to remain anonymous. This fellow has also searched the authorities without coming up with a satisfactory consensus. He seems personally to prefer the theory that hunters are to blame. I think he may be right. For some reason, the outdoorsman tends to ignore plural forms when referring to animals in the wild. "I killed two bear," he says, or "Look at all those zebra." (Sometimes, "Look at all *them* zebra.")

Harold H. Marquis of Fallbrook suggests that the angler thinks of trout and salmon as individuals. "They are not to be considered in the mass as are sardines. Hence the difference in pluralization?"

I doubt that theory. If a man who had caught six trout thought of them as individuals, which surely he would, since each one of them probably gave him a lot of trouble, he would call them "trouts," which suggests a number of individual trouts, not just a mess of fish. Thus does the aquarist refer to the specimens in his tank as fishes, not fish.

Dode Geer of Pasadena complicates the whole question by wanting to know why, if gooses are called geese, mongooses aren't called mongeese. I don't know. Mrs. Geer also wants to know why, if mouses are called mice, spouses aren't called spice. "I like spice," she adds. I do too.

Why do we call cattle and other cloven-hoofed ruminants a herd, instead of a flock or a brood? The entire question of the words given to large assemblages of animals and birds is very provocative. Fortunately, an almost complete list was left us by that remarkably curious nineteenth-century scholar, the Reverend Ebenezer Cobham Brewer, in his marvelous *Dictionary of Phrase and Fable*.

Brewer evidently had a delightful time doing his research. I marvel at the literature he must have devoured and the trips he must have undertaken to learn, for example, that an assemblage of foxes is a skulk, that many peacocks make a muster, and larks an exultation.

He also tells us that an assemblage of choughs is a chattering; of crows, a murder; of elk, a gang. What are kangaroos? A troop. And nightingales? A watch.

Goldfinches in assembly are a charm; leopards a leap; gnats a cloud. Kittens, I knew not, are a kindle. I picture the gentle Brewer on one of his walks, scaring up a clamor of rooks, a spring of teals, a congregation of plovers.

Having done all the animals, this quaint encyclopedist moved on to the worlds of things and people, establishing once and for all that a number of onions are called a rope, eggs a clutch, and bells a peal; and that a number of laborers are a gang, bishops a bench, savages a horde and angels a host.

I suppose all these matters are of no great moment. But in these times of terrorism and nuclear anxiety it might be pleasant to think of trouts and peacocks, and to sit back with a lemonade in the patio and imagine an exultation of larks exulting.

Since writing these last few paragraphs I have learned that I erred. An assemblage of larks is an *exaltation* of larks, not an exultation.

What happened, obviously, is that in reading from Dr. Brewer's list I misread the word. I have been corrected on this point by a pounce of readers.

"*Exaltation* is, I believe, the word denoting a group of larks," writes Bonita Freeman. "It has always seemed to me to describe a soaring serenity, far above a giggling gaggle of geese or even a gossiping murmuration of starlings."

As I readily concede my error, perhaps the reader will concede extenuating circumstances. First, Brewer's list is in very fine print, and the new eyeglasses I recently ordered, with a greater magnifying power in the lower bifocal, have not been delivered yet. This also, I hope, will explain any errors I make in the immediate future.

A more forceful point, I would have thought, is that exultation is very nearly as good a word for larks as exaltation. The lark, or skylark, to give the bird his full poetic name, is said to have the most beautiful voice among God's creatures. May we not imagine that, when this matchless instrument is raised in song, the skylark, hearing himself, is filled with a sense of joy, glory, triumph? That in a word he exults?

Not everyone fully agrees. "Much as I admire the Reverend Brewer's research into animal collectives," writes Arnold Hano of Laguna Beach, "either he is wrong or you have copied him wrong. It's not an exultation of larks (though why not?); it's an exaltation. And I think that's better, no matter how I may imagine larks exulting. The lifting-up sense of the word fits larks."

Oh well. Why dwell on an error when we have barely touched the surface of a fascinating subject?

Selma Hefley of Carson writes that she especially likes Brewer's watch of nightingales, noting that caged nightingales were once used as watchbirds, and somewhere, perhaps, still are; because when all is well, they sing, but "when something is afoot," they fall silent.

Mike Ferguson recalls that the noted sports columnist Red Smith once did a piece on such collective nouns, inventing a few of his own, such as a fix of gamblers, a gangle of basketball players, a conspiracy of referees and a grouse of umpires.

Charles W. Trigg and others have written about James Lipton's book, *An Exaltation of Larks, or the Venereal Game* (Grossman, 1968). The odd subtitle, he explains, refers to an archaic meaning of the word venery as "the sport of hunting." It was the hunter who first made a game of giving names to groups of animals.

Lipton himself not only collects old descriptive labels, but adds a few modern ones of his own making, such as a wrangle of philosophers, a sneer of butlers, a mass of priests, a trip of hippies, a rise of miniskirts and an unction of undertakers.

Jean Fleming of Northridge also cites Lipton, noting that a very large unction of undertakers would be called an extreme unction.

Miss Fleming points out an exquisite distinction made by Brewer. While geese are merely a gaggle on the ground, in flight they are a skein. "Beautiful," says Miss Fleming.

And from my patio, in the afternoon, I commune with a hover of hawks, a repertory of mockingbirds, and an underground of gophers.

"Recently," writes Curtis W. Gibbs of Woodland Hills, "you became involved with a peacock (peahen, peafowl), which brought to mind some questions my wife and I have been asking for years, such as what does one call a male guinea hen? A male ladybug? Or a male black widow spider?"

I don't know, and none of the several books I have referred to is of any help. Evidently the waters are too deep, and they are simply hoping that folk usage will deal with these vexing questions.

This of course has happened with peacocks, which hardly anyone calls peafowl or peahens anymore. But just the opposite seems to have happened to guinea fowl. We hear of guinea hens, but not guinea cocks, or guinea fowl. For example, if one sees a flock of these remarkable birds skittering across a road he does not cry out "Guinea fowl," whatever he observes their sex to be, but "Guinea hens!" I am only guessing, since I have never lived around guinea fowl, and if we want to know what ordinary people call things, the encyclopedias are not to be trusted.

In Africa this fowl can be depended on to gabble hysterically at the least bit of excitement, and thus is highly prized as a watchdog, or should I say watchbird. Whether it is the hen or the cock that does this, or both, I don't know.

As for the words ladybird (or ladybug) and black widow spider, they are so entrenched that one hardly thinks of there being any males at all; but of course everything in nature except rocks is either one sex or the other or both.

There hardly seems any reason to give the male black widow a name of his own, since this scrawny but virile wretch's only purpose in a very brief life is to perform his male function in the sex act—once— immediately after which, evidently having found it rather distasteful, the female kills and devours him. Of course many individual males in many species, including the human animal itself, turn out to have little more to do in life than this. But except for the male black widow, they are usually allowed to do it more than once.

I suppose some male black widows escape their mates after making love and go on to outlive them, in which case they would be black widowers, but this probably happens too rarely for the term to be generic. Anyway, a fellow willing to allow himself to be eaten, merely as the price of a single indiscretion, is too self-effacing to deserve his own name.

"And now," Gibbs continues, "my crossword puzzle dictionary informs me that a cuckoo's mate is a wryneck. This causes me to wonder which gender is the cuckoo?"

The answer to that, of course, is that crossword puzzle dictionaries are useful for working crossword puzzles, and nothing else. The cuckoo, like the peacock, guinea hen, ladybird and black widow, is either a male or a female, depending on its sex. The notion that the wryneck is a male cuckoo will be found only in crossword puzzles.

Finally, Gibbs notes that for several years a tiny bird has been charming him with a call that sounds like the name "Stewart." But lately, he observes, a mockingbird in his front yard oak tree has added "Stewart" to his vocabulary.

"I'm not a bird watcher—an observer, perhaps," Gibbs says, "but I thought you might recognize the call. Incidentally, the tiny bird enunciates better than the mocker."

Nothing in my shelf of bird lore makes note of a bird whose cry is "Stewart." Thus, I think we may conjecture that there is a bird in Gibbs's yard whose given name happens to be Stewart.

This brings to mind a strange phenomenon reported by my friend and neighbor, Dalton, in the spring of 1968, or thereabouts. He had a mockingbird that kept saying "Frederic," which is Dalton's given name.

Dalton is of the opinion that this bird has learned his name from hearing Mrs. Dalton call him in from the pool; but perhaps it was only a female cuckoo, calling to her mate.

ABLE WAS I ERE...

"But Napoleon,
he would not have say that."

The other morning as I was driving in the mountains with my French daughter-in-law, a Toyota passed us and I remembered that "a Toyota" is a palindrome.

A palindrome, of course, is a word, phrase, or sentence that reads the same forwards and backwards. The word mom is one of the simplest and most common palindromes.

It had never occurred to me that "a Toyota" was a palindrome until I received a letter from Gene Kelly of Beverly Hills, who mischievously pointed it out, thus sending me off on a palindrome chase that lasted for weeks, with sparse results.

As Kelly said, the most famous and perhaps the best palindrome in English is "Able was I ere I saw Elba," a remark attributed to Napoleon during his exile on the island of Elba.

"The greatest fun with the palindrome," according to Kelly, "is introducing it to elementary school children. . . . Try it on kids, especially the ones who like to read and spell. Don't start them out on long sentences. Introduce them to a few single words like mom and pop and they will soon come back at you with dad and tut and dud and bob and peep.... The next step would be 'Dennis sinned,' and so on."

I found that I had no great knack for the palindrome. Perhaps it's because I have a hard time thinking backwards. But there is a delight in discovering an unintentional palindrome, such as 'a Toyota,' or reading a good one somebody else has thought up.

In Brewer's dictionary I found that the longest palindrome in English is probably "Dog as a devil deified, deified lived as a god." It doesn't make a lot of sense, but perhaps it's poetry, and doesn't have to make sense.

I was thus lost in palindromes when I realized that I hadn't said a word in miles. I was afraid my daughter-in-law would think I was in a pique.

"Do you know what a palindrome is?" I asked her. I hoped the subject might give us a few miles of conversation, though I wasn't sure she'd be very good at it, English not being her native language.

"I do not know that word," she said.

I explained. "A Toyota is a palindrome. You have to put the 'a' in front of the Toyota, and then it is spelled the same way backwards and forwards."

"Ah, oui," she said. "Yes, I see."

My favorite, I told her, was what Adam said to Eve when they first met.

"He said, 'I'm Adam, madam.' "

She thought it over. "It is no good, Mr. Smith."

"What do you mean, no good? It's perfect."

"But it begins with an I and ends with an m. Right?"

Of course she was right. Something had gone wrong. I was puzzled, as well as embarrassed. It had worked all right the last time. It took me a mile to figure it out.

"I got it wrong," I said. "What Adam said was not, 'I'm Adam, madam,' but 'Madam, I'm Adam.'"

She nodded. "Ah, oui, Mr. Smith. That is better."

"The most famous palindrome of all," I said later on, hoping to repair my self-esteem," is 'Able was I ere I saw Elba.'"

"I do not understand."

"'Able was I ere I saw Elba,'" I repeated slowly. "It's what Napoleon said when he was in exile on the island of Elba." We drove on half a mile in silence.

"Mr. Smith," she said at last, "it is no good."

"What do you mean, no good?" I said. "It's perfect. It's the best palindrome in the English language."

"But Napoleon, he would not have say that."

She was right again, of course. I had always realized that the quotation must be apocryphal. Napoleon would hardly have spoken the language of his enemy. So it wasn't history. It was still an excellent palindrome.

"Well," I asked her a while later, "what do you think Napoleon would have said, under the circumstances?"

"'Je pouvais tout faire,'" she said, "'avant d'avoir vu Elbe.'"

Maybe it's history. But it's not a palindrome.

In crediting Adam with mankind's first palindrome, and one of its best, I hadn't considered that Eve might have had the last word.

"For the edification of women's libbers," wrote Norman Lessing of Santa Monica, "you might have included the typically snide female topper to the famous Adam palindrome. Their full dialogue follows:

"'Madam, I'm Adam.'

"'Eve.'"

Perhaps this was in fact the world's first conversation. If so, I don't agree that Eve's answer was snide, nor that a snide remark is "typically female." Her answer seems to me to have been admirably concise and apt, as well as a palindrome. Adam must have realized then and there that his helpmeet was a very clever creature indeed.

More light is cast on this original dialogue, however, by the linguist Dmitri A. Borgmann in his book *Language on Vacation.* Borgmann points out that the ideal rejoinder for Eve would have been, "Sir, I'm Iris." Eve might also have dropped the first and last letters of Adam's remark and said, "Adam, I'm Ada." But of course if God had wanted her to outwit Adam he would have called her Iris or Ada, instead of Eve. She did the best she could with what she had, and she has been doing it ever since.

Several readers have sent me what Borgmann calls the most felicitous palindrome in the English language, a language which, by the way, yields up few very good ones. This one is a eulogy to George Washington Goethals, builder of the Panama Canal.

"A man, a plan, a canal—Panama."

Other readers have offered "Lewd did I live and evil I did dwel." But this one requires the dropping of the final l in dwell, which a purist cannot accept.

Borgmann also cites a slight variation: "Lewd did I live and, Edna, evil I did dwel"—which is fine if you don't mind dropping the l and can imagine confessing your sins to someone named Edna.

The most provocative palindrome was sent by a man who didn't want his name used, possibly because it touches on a personal subject. It is "Sex at noon taxes."

That is not only a perfect palindrome, but also can be interpreted in either of two ways. It could mean that sex at noon is taxing, which nobody can deny; or it could refer to a tax imposed on sex at noon, which nobody wants. The legislators have left little enough of our lives untaxed.

Several persons have sent me "Yreka Bakery," and one of them, Robert Anderson of Ventura, says he saw the sign many years ago on a bakery in Yreka, up in Siskiyou County, at the top of the state of California.

"The bakery should not be difficult to find," he wrote, "and I feel assured its name has never changed during the long span of intervening years, and never will."

I wondered if it was still there. Like Anderson, I doubted that the Yreka Bakery would ever go out of business or give up a name that was so logical and unique, and a perfect palindrome. I had to find out. I dialed information for the Northern California zone.

"What town?" the operator asked.

"Yreka."

"One moment."

In a moment another operator came on. "Information."

"Is there a Yreka Bakery?" I asked.

She didn't even have to look it up. "No," she said, "there isn't."

Oh, well. The palindrome does not live by bread alone.

Then I heard from George Wacker, a Siskiyou County supervisor. "For years," he wrote, "it has been argued which was Yreka's claim to fame—discovery of gold in 1852, the vigilante hanging of four men in 1896, or the Yreka Bakery.

"The historic town boasted a bakery for approximately one hundred years—1860-1960—under the name Yreka Bakery. The bakery and Yreka received nationwide fame when Yreka Bakery appeared as a palindrome in Ripley's *Believe It Or Not*. The old bakery location now houses an art shop identified by another palindrome—Yrella Gallery."

Once more I phoned Yreka information. "Is there a Yrella Gallery?" I asked, half expecting to be let down again.

"Yes," the operator said, "one moment."

The proprietor of the Yrella Gallery turned out to be a Mrs. Bettyann Dunlap. Yes, she had taken over the old bakery on Miner Street and started the gallery five years earlier. The bakery had closed a decade before that when the old man, the last of the family, died.

"The first year," said Mrs. Dunlap, "I left the old lettering on the window—Yreka Bakery. Now I have a sign that says Yrella Gallery—formerly Yreka Bakery. The old brick oven is still here. They used to bake with coals—delicious, crunchy French bread. At least I haven't torn the oven out for the used brick."

"Who thought up the name Yrella Gallery?" I asked.

"It was all my own original idea."

"Do people know it's a palindrome?"

"Not too many. They think it's supposed to be Yreka and we spelled it wrong. They come in here every day, looking for bread."

So the palindrome lives in Yreka, believe it or not. And as for those who come to the Yrella Gallery for bread—let them eat cake.

THE QUEER OLD DEAN

In real life, a fious praud.

We recently shared a box at the Hollywood Bowl with friends and it turned out to be one of those evenings where everything seems right, from the wine to the last bravo. And I capped it with an excellent spoonerism, my first in years.

Like every good spoonerism it was unconscious, a slip of the tongue, so I am really not entitled to any credit, but it was so apt and beguiling that I will always remember it with an author's pride.

Ruth Vincent was our hostess and her other guests were Robert Nathan and his wife, Anna Lee. Mrs. Vincent had driven up from her house in Baja California, bringing fresh scallops cooked in lemon juice. My wife brought a green salad and a clutch of extremely dainty cucumber sandwiches, and the Nathans brought the wine, a Pouilly-Fumé 1969.

I have experienced nights at the Bowl that were more beautiful and moving, like the night Itzhak Perlman played a Mozart concerto under a full moon that had only recently been walked on by two Americans. That night had given me a sense of oneness with the universe; this night made me feel thirty years old again. Feeling thirty is even better than feeling as one with the universe.

The first piece on the program was a Mozart overture: brief, light, sportive. It set the tone for the evening. The conductor was Jean-Pierre Rampal, the celebrated flutist. He looked slightly dissolute and mischievous, despite his white jacket and black tie, like some not altogether trustworthy prestidigitator one might meet in a novel by Simenon. One knew we would get no solemnity from his baton.

After the Mozart, M. Rampal came out with a flute, and it turned out he was the soloist for the evening as well as the conductor. He played a Vivaldi concerto with breathtaking virtuosity, simultaneously directing the orchestra with body English.

After tumultuous applause and a brief respite offstage, he returned with Zita Carno to attempt the duo for flute and piano by Copland. The music was as wild as two bats in a cave: primitive, complex, unpredictable, exciting. There was a breeze in the Bowl and to keep his music from blowing away, Mr. Rampal had fastened it to the stand with clothespins (or what looked to me like clothespins), and occasionally the duet was suspended, Miss Carno hovering over the keyboard like a hummingbird, while the flutist reset his clothespins.

"You know," said Robert Nathan when it was over, "Copland has mad nightingales in his head."

But the apogee of the evening, and I say that even though it was followed by Beethoven's Eighth symphony, was the Concerto in G for two flutes and orchestra by Cimarosa, the Italian Mozart, in which Mr. Rampal was joined by flutist Anne Diener Giles.

"She handles her clothespins better than he does," my wife whispered as the two of them fastened their music to the racks.

It was a lovely piece, both innocent and erotic. Mr. Rampal was the satyr, Miss Giles his prey. They had met in the woods and fallen into a flirtation, talking with their flutes. But soon they were talking with their bodies, too, like two white butterflies courting—the bent knees, the outthrust hip, the provocative shoulder turned away. Was Miss Giles the seduced, I began to wonder, or the seducer? Why does the satyr always get the blame?

There were three curtain calls, cries of bravo and exuberant whistling, and a basket of flowers was thrust into Miss Giles's hands.

"She has a sweeter flute than he has," Nathan said.

Mrs. Vincent had brought along one of Nathan's books of poetry as a gift for me, and at the intermission she asked him to inscribe it. He consented, adding a new poem in his hand:

> *I chose the high and lonely path*
> *Far up above the common lot.*
> *And so the lowliest poet hath*
> *What I have not.*

"I call it Fame," he said. "I wrote it just this morning. I had this picture of myself walking on a high wire, and suddenly there was no wire there."

Robert Nathan has nightingales in his head, but they aren't mad, they're merely enchanted.

After the concert we were trudging up the asphalt toward the car when I caught sight of Miss Giles a few steps ahead of me. She was laughing and tossing her long blond hair, and a girl was a step behind her with her basket of flowers. I hurried up to catch her; I had to let her know how I felt about her. But she is a leggy young woman, and I was burdened with a picnic basket on each arm. She got away.

I turned around to go back to my group. Nathan was right behind me. The others were out of sight in the crowd.

"What happened to you?" my wife asked when we found them.

"I was trying to catch Miss Giles," I replied.

We had said goodnight to the others and were on our way home when I remembered what Nathan had said about Miss Giles.

"She has a fluter sweet than he has," I said.

It was a lovely spoonerism, I thought, though technically imperfect, and my wife didn't laugh. She understood me perfectly.

"By the way," writes Swend C. Rasmussen of Huntington Beach, "what is a spoonerism?"

I was hoping someone would ask. It is with pleasure that I am able to recall one of history's most amusing gentlemen. Perhaps the simplest way to introduce him is to quote his entry in *Webster's Biographical Dictionary:*

> **Spooner, William Archibald.** 1844-1930. Anglican clergyman and educator; dean (1876-89) and warden (1903-24), of New College, Oxford. An occasional lapse of speech, whereby he transposed sounds in two or more words (as a blushing crow, for a crushing blow), led to coinage of the word *spoonerism* in the English language.

Spooner is also the subject of a paragraph in Brewer's dictionary, which quotes two of the finest examples of his work:

"We all know what it is," he once told his doubtless rapt audience, "to have a half-warmed fish within us." He meant, we must assume, "a half-formed wish."

Brewer's also cites Spooner's famous evangelical affirmation, "Yes, indeed; the Lord is a shoving leopard," along with his announcement in church that the next hymn would be "kinkering Kongs their titles take."

Of course Spooner neither invented the spoonerism nor did he hold a copyright. Brewer's defines spoonerism as "a ludicrous form of metathesis that consists of transposing the initial sounds of words so as to form some laughable combination." Metathesis was around long before Spooner, just as malapropisms were in abundance long before the prolific Mrs. Malaprop came along to give them her name.

The spoonerism and its namesake are allotted half a page in *The People's Almanac* (Doubleday), by Wallechinsky and Wallace, the entry being a reprint from *Human Words* (Chilton), by Robert Hendrickson.

Hendrickson gets into the spirit of the task by introducing Spooner as "a learned man, but not spell woken...." He notes Spooner was wont to metathesize in church, where he once told a lady (it is said), "Mardon me padam, this pie is occupued; allow me to sew you to another sheet."

Such a complex spoonerism is obviously not beyond human ingenuity, since it does exist. Doubtless, though, it is not the genuine article, but an imitation conceived by some admirer of the old gentleman and fraudulently attributed to him.

I am also skeptical of several others Hendrickson cites. Once in the classroom, for example, Spooner is said to have confronted a student with the accusation, "You hissed my mystery lesson." That just might be true. I'm not so sure about his supposed dismissal of another student with the words, "You have deliberately tasted two worms and can leave Oxford by the town drain." (I suppose he meant the down train to London.)

It is perhaps fortunate for us that his peculiar talent is one that may not deteriorate with age. Some of his best, in fact, occurred in his later years. During World War I, for example, he is said to have told the home front, "When the boys come back from France, we'll have the hags flung out!" Also, he once eulogized Queen Victoria as "our queer old dean." That is another one I like to think of as genuine.

Probably almost everyone hears or commits a spoonerism every day. Some of them fall so easily from the tongue, making their own kind of sense, that they go unnoticed. The best of all are those a speaker makes in front of a large audience, and these are especially precious, for some reason, when nobody seems to have caught them but oneself.

This gratifying experience was once the lot of Alfred Conner Bowman of Hermosa Beach, and though it occurred forty years ago, he still remembers it with bliss. Melvin Purvis, then the FBI's No. 2 gangbuster and a national hero, was the speaker at a meeting of the County Bar Association in Los Angeles. "The chairman for the evening gave him the usual extravagant buildup," Bowman recalls, "culminating in his introduction to the assembly, loud and clear, as Mervin Pelvis!"

"You have unleashed a darking bog," writes Janice Lester of Santa Monica. "The best spoonerism I ever heard was uttered by Roger Johnson in admiration of Carson McCullers' *The Salad of the Bad Cafe.*"

"My favorite," writes Barb Tiffany of Rancho Palos Verdes, "was uttered by Deems Taylor, American composer, writer of books about music and commentator on the New York Philharmonic radio programs. He made a slip of the tongue during intermission at the Hollywood Bowl, and then said, 'That reminds me of the time when I was talking at a Jerome Kern memorial concert and climaxed my speech by saying, "And I, too, am a Fern Kan." ' "

"Oddly enough," writes Raymond G. Mahoney of Tucson, "probably the tops of them all, and the least quoted, was heard by at least fifteen million people on a television broadcast of a world's championship fight at Madison Square Garden some fifteen to twenty years ago. I have never heard or read a reference to it since, despite hundreds of reporters being present.

"Our good friend Jimmy Powers was announcing and there was a considerable delay before the principals climbed into the ring. Mr. Powers decided to give a little local color to fill in the gap, and started reeling off names and remarks about the bigwigs present in the ringside seats. After reeling off a dozen or so he let go with this one: 'I see the beautiful Mrs. DePuyster Van Courtland looking gorgeous in her stunning white gownless evening strap.' "

A glimpse of the Reverend Mr. Spooner as he was in real life is provided by Joan Morgens of Redlands, who had the extraordinary experience of meeting the queer old dean when she was a child.

As warden of New College, Oxford, Miss Morgens writes, Spooner was obliged occasionally to inspect the college's ecclesiastical properties in the small village of Bucknell, Oxfordshire, where her father was a rector. "It would probably have been in the summer of 1922," she recalls, "when I was ten years old, that the distinguished clergyman was coming for luncheon and to inspect the fabric of our house, barn and stables. I was determined to stay close to him so that I would not miss the spoonerisms as they were produced.

"A child's presence in the dining room while the adults enjoyed their ample luncheon was out of the question. But as soon as the inspection commenced I dogged the footsteps of the visitor as he made his rounds.

"This true story tapers off without a climax. My sharp ears heard not one spoonerism. My diligence was rewarded in the end only by this sharp remark from the old gentleman: 'Why are you following me around, little girl? Go away.' "

As Miss Morgens says, that was a long time ago, and she was only a child. What the Reverend Mr. Spooner really said, perhaps, was "Why are you gollowing me around, little firl? Woe a gay."

Anyway, I almost wish I hadn't heard the story. I am lo set down to find that our dear old queen was in real life a fious praud, a greevish pouch and a fopish old wasp.

THE DECLARATIVE QUESTION

What Adam and Eve really said.

I have been asked by Gordon Turner of Huntington Beach to comment on what he calls the Declarative Question.

"A perfect example," he writes, "is in the TV commercial, wherein a lady's voice is heard over the speaker system in a restaurant: 'Attention! There's a Datsun B210 in the parking lot? With its lights on?'

"Or a voice on the phone says, 'Hello. This is Jim Jones? The TV repairman?'

"How say you?"

I don't know whether there is another term for this phenomenon, but Declarative Question seems good enough. We are all familiar with this trick and use it, though I don't think it's a trend, as Turner suggests, so much as a well-established form that has recently become more noticeable, thanks to electric sound systems that spread every usage faster and farther than simple conversation used to do.

Actually the Declarative Question is a very effective form of condensation, and shows how clever we human beings are at language. Even a person without literary training performs a remarkable bit of telescoping when he says, "This is Jim Jones? The TV repairman?"

What he is really saying is, "This is Jim Jones. Do you remember the name? I'm the TV repairman. The one that fixed your Zenith? Last summer?"

And of course, "Attention! There's a Datsun B210 in the parking lot? With its lights on?" means "There's a Datsun B210 in the parking lot with its lights on. Think now, does anyone out there on the dance floor own a Datsun B210? And if so, is it possible that you left the lights on? Because if you did, you know, your battery will run down? And you won't be able to start your car?"

It is interesting that Turner finds this device only in spoken English. Perhaps that is because tradition does not allow the writer to put the question mark at the end of such a sentence, as in "This is Jim Jones?" (Though John O'Hara did it.) So he is obliged to suggest the inflection with some awkward piece of description. We are always reading something like this: " 'Hello,' he said. 'This is Jim Jones.' The way he said it, it was more a question than a statement, as if he wasn't sure of himself, and didn't expect her to remember that night in Naples..."

The Declarative question shows how much the voice can do to impart meanings that go beyond those explicit in the spoken word.

As I say, I suspect that Turner's Declarative Question is not new, but as old as language itself. I have an idea that the very first words spoken by one human being to another were a Declarative Question. As we noted earlier, Adam, on arising that fateful morning with an inexplicable pain in his side, and on being inexplicably confronted by a fully unclothed woman, was gentleman enough to remember his manners, introducing himself with the words:

"Madam, I'm Adam."

This is what modern speculative history tells us, pointing out, of course, that the first sentence formed by the human tongue, unless Adam talked to himself before Eve appeared, was a perfect palindrome.

But because that story has been presented to us mostly in writing, we are not sure how Adam handled his remark vocally. What was his inflection? What was his true meaning? Surely in a situation fraught with such uncertainties, a man or ordinary clay, like the rest of us, would not have been entirely able to hide his astonishment and fear. Try to imagine being a full-grown man and walking up to find your very first woman standing at your side, with her rompers off. We can be sure that he did not say simply, "Madam, I'm Adam." What he said, no doubt, and shakily too, was "Madam, I'm Adam?"

And what he meant, of course, was, "Madam, my name is Adam. I don't know if you're going to believe that, because I don't know if I'm Adam myself. How could I? I never had a father and mother. I just made it up. You like it? Well, if we're going to have a meaningful relationship we might as well get on with it. What's your name?"

And Eve is supposed to have said, "Eve," which is also a perfect palindrome, though not as clever as Adam's.

But I doubt that Eve said that. My guess is that she said, "I'm hungry?" Of course I'm not supposed to put that question mark after a declarative sentence, so I would have to write it this way:

"I'm hungry," Eve said, her voice rising as if it was a question; but Adam knew, instinctively, that it wasn't. "What she really means," he thought, "is that she wants something to eat and she wants it now."

It was the first command he had ever heard, except when God spoke to him in his dreams about being fruitful, whatever that meant.

That's how it all began?

"Will you please," asks Gene De Loach of Marina del Rey, "comment on the Irrelevant Response?"

By Irrelevant Response, Mrs. De Loach explains, she means a statement that does not seem to be related to the simple question it purports to answer. This common phenomenon is also known by the Latin phrase *non sequitur*, which means simply "it does not follow."

"I refer in particular," Mrs. De Loach goes on, "to the shopkeeper whom you approach with a request: Why can't he say 'Yes' or 'No'? Seems to be impossible. Yesterday morning I took some shirts in quest of buttonholes into a shop and explained the problem, ending with 'Can you do the buttonholes?' The answer was 'She'll be back next week.'"

That certainly appears to be an excellent example of the form, but of course Mrs. De Loach came off better than I would have expected, asking such a question. If I took a shirt in and asked for buttonholes

I know what they'd say to me: "What do you mean buttonholes? Nobody does buttonholes anymore. What do you think this is? A sweatshop?"

At least there is some vague promise in "She'll be back next week." It may appear to be a non sequitur, quite unrelated to the question; yet, if she'll be back next week, whoever she is, there is hope that she can do the buttonholes. But evidently Mrs. De Loach didn't have that much faith or was in too much of a hurry.

"Taking that answer as a negative," she says, "I went to another shop whre a man listened to my request sullenly, then looked at me and said, 'Edith!' He then disappeared and a young girl came out, looked critically at the shirts and silently placed pins in them. Still saying nothing to me, she took the shirts to a machine, and while chatting gaily with a girlfriend, put in the buttonholes, and then spoke her first word to me: 'Dollar forty.' "

It seems to me that Mrs. De Loach came off fairly well, non sequiturs or not. She got her buttonholes, a miracle in itself, and at what seems to me a very modest price for these times.

It is even more interesting, though, that the shop-keeper and his assistant performed this rare service for Mrs. De Loach with the expenditure of only three words between them—"Edith!" and "Dollar forty." That seems to be to be an example of communication reduced to its bones, which, in the age of the talk show, is almost as obsolete an art as buttonholes.

HAVE A NICE DAY

"See ya later, alligator."

I can think of no other phrase or expression that has gained such currency in American speech in recent years as "Have a nice day."

Of course it isn't as pervasive as the mindless interjection "You know," or "Y'know," without which, what is left of conversation on and off the television talk show would collapse.

But "Have a nice day" at least has the distinction of being a true sentence. It has the appearance of making sense, even though it may be only an idle expression of good will without much assurance of fulfillment.

I wondered if I was the only person who had doubts about "Have a nice day," but a reader named Carol D. Clark writes that her own reaction is something stronger than mere doubt.

"How about saying a few unkind words," she suggests, "about the clerks, gas station attendants, and other total strangers who feel obligated (or maybe instructed) to tell every customer to 'have a nice day . . . nice evening . . . nice weekend . . .' or whatever.

"It's one thing if they know you personally, but quite another if they are unaware of your circumstances. Maybe you just lost your job, had a death in the family, were summoned to court, are coming down with the flu. . . . In any of these or similar situations it seems very presumptuous to tell a person to 'have a nice day, now.' Am I just an old crank or do other people feel the same way?"

Robert G. Adair of Santa Ana also deplores the epidemic spread of "Have a nice day" and its cousins, which he calls "The Indifferent Imperative."

"My almost daily exposure to these dreadful things begins with my leave-taking of the chap at our neighborhood Shell station," he says, "or of the clerk at the dry cleaners. 'Have a nice day,' they direct. And most every day I receive a dozen or so of these by telephone. Never a wish or a hope—just have it. The next lot comes with luncheon. From the dining room's host or hostess: 'Have a good meal,' or, a fascinating variation, 'Enjoy your lunch.' "

"Have a nice day" has become so common that I can hardly remember what we said before it came along. Its function, of course, is simply to end some everyday human transaction—social or business— on a note of good will and Godspeed. But it has become so pervasive, so automatic, that one is neither surprised nor heartened to hear it anymore. It means no more than the listless "Thank you" recited by the person at the cash register who hands out your change while looking slightly past your left ear. (This bit of business has apparently been imported from France, where it is de rigueur, especially for American tourists.)

What did we used to say? The most popular phrase,

as I remember, was "So long." H. L. Mencken says so long has been attributed to the German *so lange* and even the Yiddish *shalom*. But in fact it is English and not even an Americanism, though Walt Whitman used it in a poem a century ago, and in my schooldays it was standard. (William Safire discusses "Have a nice day" in *On Language*, an amiable treasure chest of contemporary usage, noting that etymologists have traced it all the way back to Chaucer, who wrote the line, in *The Canterbury Tales*, "Fare wel, have good day.")

We also used to say "See you later," or "See ya later," which in the 1950s gave birth to "See ya later, alligator." This in turn led to "In a while, crocodile," but that one never really caught on.

In the 1960s, with the growing distate for the Vietnam war, some people parted by reviving the archaic "peace." It is still heard, but "peace" has a forlorn ring to it these days and is more likely to inspire sullen laughter than hope.

Friends part with the injunction to "Take it easy," but this implies that the person told to take it easy is inclined to be reckless and foolish, and is being urged to curb wanton impulses. It merely confuses strangers.

Unfortunately, English has no counterpart for the musical *auf wiedersehen*, the elegant *au revoir*, or the lilting *hasta la vista*.

We have *goodbye*, but unlike those European phrases, it sounds rather final. There is a cold wind in it. Some people never say goodbye, for fear of tempting fate. It has an echo of that appalling word coined by one of our cemeteries to describe its service—*foreverness*.

Rather than rush into foreverness, I think I prefer

to have one nice day at a time. So I'm not usually upset when someone tells me to have a nice day. I'd rather be told to have a nice day than be ignored. The phrase has become so standard, in fact, that if a clerk or hostess neglects to say "Have a nice day" when we finish our transaction, I am sometimes a bit put out, and it causes me not to have a nice day.

On the other hand, even now, a young person can tell me to have a nice day with such an appearance of sincerity, fraudulent or not, looking me in the eye with a mixture of concern and good will, not to say affection, that I do indeed feel encouraged to go out and have a nice day, and sometimes do.

But I'm not sure that I still respond so positively to "Enjoy your lunch," or "Enjoy your dinner" as when they first appeared. The first few times I heard that imperative it did not sound mechanical or indifferent. I remember thinking how nice it was of the hostess to remind us that the purpose of dining out was to nourish the spirit as well as the flesh, and that the management wished to elicit nothing more than our pleasure. Then when the waitress said it, too, after serving the entrée, I didn't mind the repetition. It came, after all, from a young lady I already thought of almost as a friend, since she had introduced herself by saying, "Hi, I'm Cindy. I'll be your waitress."

The injunction to enjoy your dinner is not so reassuring, though, when it is tacked on at the end of an announcement such as the following, usually delivered with the soup: "Here's your soup. OK? I'm going on my break now. Your waitress will be Kathy. OK? Enjoy your lunch?"

You feel abandoned, and especially so when the promised Kathy fails to appear, evidently being on her break too, or unaware that she has been designated to bat for Cindy. When Kathy shows up, by the way, usually just in time to hand you the wrong bill, I never know which young lady to tip, and usually compromise by leaving enough for both.

I have noticed, however, that sometimes when I finish my meal after one of these bad hand-offs from Cindy to Kathy, neither of them turns up to say "Have a nice day," and I leave the cash register feeling shortchanged without that customary blessing, like a man who goes out on a rainy day without his hat and his wife's perfunctory kiss. Have we actually become dependent on these indifferent imperatives—even as we resent them?

I happen to like waitresses, generally, and I am more than happy to give up the sullen perfection of the old-time professional male waiter for the winsome but unpredictable young coffee shop waitress who may be casual to a fault, but nevertheless gives a touch of personal warmth, like a sister, even if the soup is cold.

We had an extraordinary waitress the other evening, for example, when my wife and I took our younger son and his two children to a coffee shop for dinner. The waitress entered right into the family. She not only told the children what they should eat but advised me to take the fried chicken, and when I stood up to leave—after laying down a handsome but well-deserved tip—she had the temerity to give me a friendly elbow in the rib and a peck on the cheek, though it was more of a feint than a real kiss.

"Have a nice evening, Mr. Smith," she said with a charming French accent.

Of course she happened to be my daughter-in-law.

THE INTERROGATIVE PUTDOWN

"This is chicken?"

In our concern with the Declarative Question, the Irrelevant Response and the Indifferent Imperative—common rhetorical devices identified and named by three different readers—we have overlooked another common vehicle of speech that is related to the Declarative Question but differs from it in character and purpose.

The Declarative Question is good-natured and helpful. Its character is diffidence; its purpose is to give useful information. ("This is Jim Jones? The TV repairman?") But the character of its cousin, which we now consider, is false innocence, and its purpose is ridicule and dominance.

The form has been identified by R. W. Prouty of Westlake Village, who defines it as "a Question-Statement that is much used by people in positions of authority (including wives and mothers).

"I first realized this," he explains, "in a high school woodworking class when one of the students cut the tip of his finger off with a power saw. The instructor rushed over and asked, 'Why did you do that?' What he really meant, of course, was 'That was a stupid thing to do.'

"This Question-Statement does not require an answer, but most of us try anyway. Fortunate is he who has a valid and believable response ready. . . . It seems to me that personal relationships are often strained by the use of this type of question."

Of course this form is so familiar that more examples than those Prouty has supplied are hardly needed. I think, though, that Prouty's term—the Question-Statement—is inadequate to suggest its underlying wickedness. Perhaps it could more accurately be called the Interrogative Putdown.

Certainly it is among the most common of weapons, and is especially useful in situations where one wishes to demoralize an adversary—often a loved one—without seeming to have meant any harm.

The Interrogative Putdown is known to every married couple, I suspect, and is perhaps more often employed by those who are generally on good terms with one another than by those who are not. Those who quarrel openly have no need for the disguised thrust of the Interrogative Putdown.

It is a sign of our mutual affection, I would say, and not a symptom of some submerged hostility, that my wife almost always resorts to the Interrogative Putdown to let me know that I have done something stupid, such as driving past our turnoff on the freeway again. What she usually says is: "Where are you going?"

This suggests genuine curiosity. She had been expecting me to take the usual turnoff but I have gone past it, and now, excited by the prospect of adventure, she simply can't wait to find out where

I'm taking her. How exciting, she seems to imply, to have an unpredictable mate!

Of course I know the old Interrogative Putdown when I hear it. I'm not fooled by its mask of innocence. What she really means is, "Well, you've done it again, boy. You really are getting absentminded."

Naturally she doesn't wish to come right out and say I'm getting absentminded, because absentminded is a code word for senile, which ordinary kindness does not allow her to say. So she simply says, "Where are you going?" and the message is received.

I'm afraid I do the same thing, especially in matters of the table. She is a good cook: not showy, not fussy, but good, and she is willing to experiment and risk disaster. But she has her pride.

For example, just the other evening I asked her, after sampling an unfamiliar dish: "This is *chicken?*"

I'm sure she recognized it at once as an Interrogative Putdown, meaning that I knew very well it was chicken but I didn't like the way it was prepared and I didn't want her to try it again.

Her answer was very clever; neither openly resentful nor belligerent, yet it offered me no recognizable advantage, no chance for a follow-up. She might have said, for example, "What do you think it is?" That would have been a Counter-Interrogative Putdown, meaning "Are you such a clod you don't know chicken when you taste it?"

But of course that would have given me an excellent opening. "Marinated herring?" I might have asked, which would have been a Counter-Counter-Interrogative Putdown, meaning "This chicken is so bad it tastes like herring." Two Interrogative Putdowns in a row, unblocked, are usually enough to achieve the desired result, which is to establish one's superiority for the remainder of the evening.

But alas, what she actually said was: "Does the stereo really have to be that loud?"

Simply brilliant. Not only was it a Counter-Interrogative Putdown, meaning "Are you deaf?" (i.e., senile) but a non sequitur as well. The old one-two.

There was nothing to do but turn down the stereo and eat my dinner. Whatever it was.

To the Interrogative Putdown and other conversational devices we have examined here, Ralph Viggers of Ontario would like to add what he calls "the self-effacing statement designed to elicit compliments."

That is rather a verbose description of a very common device that all of us have heard and most of us have practiced. I can't think of any way of summing it up in a word or two, unless we call it the "Shucks, ma'am" opening.

This phrase derives, of course, from that standard scene in old westerns where the hero, on being embraced by some toothsome female for saving her life and honor, looks down at his boots and drawls, "Shucks, ma'am, twarn't nothin'."

I imagine that very line, word for word, was delivered by at least two generations of horse-opera heroes, from Hoot Gibson to Jimmy Stewart. In fact, if it hadn't been a cliché already when he first said it, you might think the line had been written especially for Stewart. He could turn a line like that into an Academy Award nomination.

I'm not quite as cynical about it as Viggers. Sometimes the self-effacing remark was truly ingenuous.

Our hero was indeed a modest fellow, and he regarded his exploits as nothing more than what should be expected of a man confronted by a lady in distress.

A modest demeanor used to be so generally admired in our heroes that we found it not only in westerns but also in more sophisticated movies, and finally in real life, which has always copied its manners from the movies in America.

One of the finest self-deprecatory lines ever delivered in the movies, I believe, was spoken in "Samson and Delilah" by Victor Mature, whose gifts did not include the ability to project modesty. As Samson, Mature is riding through the desert in a chariot with Hedy Lamarr when suddenly their path is blocked by a snarling lion. Mature hops down from the chariot, much like a man getting out of a car to fix a flat, and wrestles the lion to death while Miss Lamarr watches, one slender hand against her slender throat. When Mature hops back into the chariot Miss Lamarr (who later cuts his hair off) says something like, "You might have been hurt!"

"Shucks, ma'am," says Mature, "It was only a young lion." (I don't believe he actually said "Shucks, ma'am," since it was an eastern, or Middle Eastern, not a western, but the tone was the same.)

Of course the 1920s produced a pantheon of modest heroes, of whom the most exemplary was Charles Lindberg. It is said that, on arriving in Paris after his historic nonstop flight from New York, and finding fifty million Frenchmen at his feet, the Lone Eagle asked only for a glass of milk.

Modesty was in fact so unrelentingly expected of our heroes that all the great champions of the 1920s and 1930s seem to have been as shy and self-effacing as Easter bunnies, despite persuasive evidence that to be a champion of anything requires a superabundance of ego.

Bobby Jones, Jack Dempsey, Helen Wills—killers, all; but they rarely said in public what they must have felt—that they were the greatest. Even Bill Tilden, the Hamlet of the tennis courts, was awfully nice about complimenting his opponents for good shots: "Good shot, Fred!" he might shout, or "Oh, George—peach!" as a rare service ace blew by him. Imagine a line like that coming from Jimmy Connors or John McEnroe today.

Even Babe Ruth, who had so much ego it came out of his pores like the beer he drank before games, was modest of speech in public. Only by a special dispensation, something like the divine right of kings, was he cheered, instead of booed, for pointing into the bleachers to call his shot in the 1932 World Series.

And Gene Tunney, when he outlasted Dempsey (with the help of the referee), was smart enough not to say, "I'm the greatest!" He was already disliked for bringing down a man the country had begun to love only when he fell, and any gloating on his part would have got him pilloried, at least, and possibly deported. He was regarded as a foreigner, anyway, because he was reputed to quote Shakespeare.

So the day of the self-effacing hero is past. The Shucks, ma'am, is heard no more. Our champions strut, brag, and play to the grandstand with spiked footballs and end-zone dances. They dislike their fans and bad-mouth their employers and honor only their agents.

Actually, I don't mind. They have, as Tunney would have said, but an hour upon the stage and then are heard no more. Let them strut. The exuberant demonstrations of wide receivers who have just left their last would-be tacklers flat on their faces are part of the game today, and fun to see. Now that he has fallen, who begrudges Muhammad Ali his posturing? He was indeed, for a time, the greatest.

But shucks, who would agree with my poor scribblings?

"I enjoyed your article on the declarative question, but with some reservation," writes Ezra Wyeth of Northridge, "since you may have been guilty of using the unidentified *we*—a practice that can be both confusing to the reader and obnoxious."

Quoting from that article, Wyeth shows that I used *we* in various ways, switching without explanation from one to another, so that it was not exactly clear to him whom I meant by *we* in each instance.

"You began," he points out, "with 'Just the other day we dealt here . . .' You and who else?"

That's an easy one. That *we* of course meant me and those readers who had taken part in our discussion of the Declarative Question by writing letters. Certainly it was their comments that shed the most light on the subject, and it would have been unworthy of me to imply that I had dealt with it all by myself.

Later on, Wyeth notes, I seemed to be referring to some other *we* when I said, "Have we actually become dependent on these Indifferent Imperatives?"

In that case my *we* meant all of us—all members of our society who either employ or are the beneficiaries of what one reader called the Indifferent Imperative, such as "Have a nice day ."

"Finally," Wyeth points out, "you went to dinner as part of another we."

Yes—that *we* was my wife and me.

So in that space of a few paragraphs I used *we* to mean three very different entities; and Wyeth is quite right. It was a bad piece of work: careless and indefensible. While each usage is proper enough in its own right, it was asking too much of the reader to guess which one I had in mind in each instance, especially since I kept switching about.

However, it wasn't as bad as it's possible to be with that veritable pronoun. As Wyeth notes, "The use of *we* has a long tradition and important people use it. The Queen of England does. So do his Holiness the Pope, and the President of the United States. Newspaper editors use it. Many teachers do: 'Children, do we have to go to the bathroom?' Nurses are addicted to it: 'We have to take our medicine now.'"

Not being a teacher, a nurse, an editor, the President of the United States, the Pope, or the Queen of England, I am fairly safe from using *we* in the pedagogical, clinical, presidential, papal or royal sense.

I would also like to say that I have never used the personal *we* in the manner to which many newspaper writers, and others given to loosing their unsolicited opinions on a beleaguered public, are addicted. That is the so-called editorial *we*, whose only function is to escape that use of *I*, which is thought too egotistical. But *I* is honest. If you're going to say something you should take the whole responsibility for it, and not try to lay it off on some nonexistent accomplice under the shelter of a *we*.

Even if I were tempted to use the editorial *we*, I would be discouraged by the thought that Queen Victoria, upon seeing an imitation of herself by her groom-in-waiting, is said to have declared: "We are not amused."

Though she sat on the throne for sixty years that was the only remark of Victoria's considered worth including in Bartlett's *Familiar Quotations*, where it resides in regal splendor to this day.

It is my opinion that in the light of Queen Victoria's historic preemption of *we* in a context of theatrical criticism, it is vain and presumptuous of a mere newspaper columnist or critic to use it himself, when a simple modest *I* will do.

There is of course the other kind of editorial *we*, which is found in newspaper editorials and not under a writer's byline. This *we*, as I suppose almost everyone knows, means the editors who constitute the paper's philosophical hierarchy, and it implies that the opinions ascribed to it represent their consensus, or at least their interpretation of the publisher's opinion. I have never used that *we*, never having been invited to input into our hierarchy's output.

Even if I were not inhibited by the Victorian preemption, I would never use *we* when I meant myself alone, for fear some frivolous observation of mine might be misunderstood as the consensus of our editors. I do not wish to write "We are not amused," for example, only to get a memo from our hierarchy saying, "Neither are we."

I apologize to Wyeth for my ambiguity, and if he wishes to persist in trying to decipher these reflections, I will clarify my *we* right now.

When I say *we* I mean either me and those who take part in the forum, me and some other designated group (the U.S. Marines), me and the rest of humanity, or me and my wife.

And once in a whole, of course, I mean me and Humpty-Dumpty.

PULLET SURPRISES

*It's time for
youth in Asia.*

The other day a young woman who was visiting in our living room brought the conversation around to one of her children, a daughter who was evidently quite bright and doing well in school.

"You know," she told us, with a flush of pride, "they've put her in an exhilarated class."

"That sounds wonderful," I said, thinking how exciting it must be to study in an atmosphere of exhilaration.

Then the mother went on talking about her daughter's work and finally I realized it was an *accelerated* class the child was in, not exhilarated. Mentally, I gave our visitor a Pullet Surprise.

I hadn't even known of the Pullet Surprise until a few years earlier when Eula Greene Miller, then living in Laguna Hills, sent me a copy of a paperback book written by her late sister, Amsel Greene.

Pullet Surprises (now long out of print) is a collection of malapropisms and other unintentional but marvelous word misuses by teenage students. It owes its title to a high school boy who wrote, "In 1937, Eugene O'Neill won a Pullet Surprise."

"Here was the term," Amsel Greene wrote in her preface, "for which I had been groping. As the teacher of a high school course in vocabulary building, I had jotted down hundreds of classroom misinterpretations for which I had found no name. The terms boners, bloopers and booboos imply stupidity or inadvertence, whereas student errors are often marvels of ingenuity and logic.

"But Pullet Surprises sparked a Eureka response. Its rightness had the impact of revelation!"

Miss Greene offered her collection not in ridicule but in wonder and delight, and acknowledged her debt to the students "who met the challenge of unknown words with a logic and an ingenuity that made misinterpretation truly admirable."

Thus, she happily awarded Pullet Surprises to students who used such words as derelict, amnesia, cursory, diffident and cynic in the following imaginative ways.

"We found it hard to understand his Scottish derelict." ... "The doctor said to take some milk of amnesia." ... "Fred's mother used to wash out his mouth with soap to curb his cursory tendencies." ... "He expects to retire and live on his diffidence." ... "The Rocky Mountain road was the most cynic of our trip."

Miss Greene made a noble attempt to analyze and categorize the various types of Pullet Surprises, but this was not entirely successful. Mostly, they are just good reading. On one page, for example, I was enchanted to find that soldiers of high rank wear opulents on their shoulders, and that space flying may be affected by comic rays.

I also read of a man who drove a red Chivalry, and a woman who wore a single pedant on a gold chain. I found out that Moses went up on Mt. Cyanide to get the Ten Commandments; about the vassal that held three barrels of beer, the banker's money that was well infested, the father whose inspiration and affluence had guided a child's whole life, and a young woman who was always making social plunders.

You can see that, as Miss Greene observed, there is a kind of inspired logic in Pullet Surprises.

I met such interesting characters as Aunt Phoebe, a matriculate housekeeper; and Mr. Graham, the local weather procrastinator. Also the generous young man who gave his fiancé a choice between a ruby and an atheist; Ted, who was good at multiplication and derision; and another chap who liked any kind of camisole dish.

Pullet Surprises often carry factual information unobtainable elsewhere. Did you know that every state is permitted to send two centaurs to Congress? That in the Sarah Desert they travel by Camelot? That geography was invented by Eucalyptus?

Some of the best Pullet Surprises conjure up fantastic visions. Picture a castle with a moat full of polyglots; the forest of redwoods noted for their senility; the quaint little shop in London's Pecadillo.

Only in Pullet Surprises can you learn that a monetary is where monks live; an antithesis is something given before surgery; and a paradox is a lovely place to go when you die.

I found it all accelerating.

After my belated discovery of Pullet Surprises, I not only was divulged with malapropisms sent by my readers, but I also learned more about Miss Greene, a rare and unsung teacher who deserved a Pullet Surprise herself. For a quarter of a century, Miss Greene taught English and vocabulary in Helena, Montana, and over the years she insidiously collected the ingenious and ingenuous word misuses with which her students pervaded her—virtuously on a silver patter.

It was after she retarded and moved to Laguna Hills to live with her sister on her penchant and her diffidence, that she decided to put her Pullet Surprises into book form, just for friends. The sisters worked on the book together. Suddenly, "in the mist of battle," as one of her students had written, Miss Greene learned that she had cancer. She was given two months to live. Against this deadline the sisters speeded up their work. Perhaps sustained by the work itself, Miss Greene lived eighteen months.

The sisters were not sophisticated in the ways of publishing. Anyway, there was no time to make the rounds, trying to find a publisher. They found a printer in Fullerton and had 3,000 copies of *Pullet Surprises* printed at their own expense. These went into their garage. A few hundred were taken by bookstores in Helena. Friends bought a few hundred more. Just before she died, Miss Greene signed a contract with Scott Foresman, a textbook publisher that sold mainly to schools. Few *Pullet Surprises* reached stores or the public.

Later Mrs. Miller sent a copy to Ralph Story, a popular Los Angeles television figure, and he told his listeners about the book on his morning show. "The astonishing and delightful result," said Eula Miller, "was that within the month we sold the 650 copies we had left in the garage."

Meanwhile, the indefatigable Mrs. Malaprop's chickens are still coming home to roast.

Ted Kopacki of Anaheim writes of the student who defined "vestal," as in vestal virgin, as "pure and chased." This is a true Pullet Surprise. There is no merit in purity if the virgin has not been chased.

Ferrell Burton of Pacific Palisades writes of having just returned from Switzerland, where he climbed the Matador. Emily Murphy of Yorba Linda has a gossipy neighbor who told about the local man who had committed stationary rape. "To this day ," adds Mrs. Murphy, "I have never been able to get a true mental picture of that event."

Whatever my intellectual shortcomings, I do have a good ear for double-entendre and the vocabulary of sex, even when the words are misspelled; so I am embarrassed that I didn't immediately get the meaning of the phrase sex phine, written by an eighth-grade girl about a classmate whose yearbook she was signing.

This lapse occurred when I was quoting a few of the inscriptions in the yearbook of a boy who graduated from Richard Henry Dana Junior High School, Arcadia, in 1964. Cathy Carnahan of San Clemente, the boy's mother, had been overcome by nostalgia as the commencement season neared, and peeked into her son's old book to recapture the flavor of that time.

Among the several inscriptions she sent me was this one: "To the biggest sex phine I know—B.B."

"Sex phine?" she said. "My eighth-grader? Who was only interested in football and track and baseball in those days?"

And I wrote: "Alas, I also am innocent of the

meaning of sex phine, but whatever it is, it evidently occurs earlier than mothers think." (The irony of it is that I was a sex phine myself in junior high school. I would have recognized the term instantly, I believe, if I hadn't pronounced the *i* as in fine, instead of as in machine.)

Of the numerous explanations I have received since, perhaps the simplest is this one from Elizabeth Farrar of Hemet. "Sex phine is easy: sex fiend. If you had read thousands of essays, all spelling would be understandable. I had a student once who spoke of her pheonce."

"Can't you see," writes Arthur Dowling of Manhattan Beach, "that sex phine rhymes with Josephine?"

Most of the letters are from English teachers, or former English teachers, whose eyes and ears have been conditioned to interpret such aberrant spellings as phine for fiend and pheonce for fiance.

"My own favorite student effort in this vein," Rose Martz of Upland adds, "was an essay entitled 'Youth in Asia,' a description of student life in China. Of course the assigned topic was Euthanasia."

All this may seem of small importance, but I happen to have a very personal reason for being concerned over my failure to recognize the meaning of sex phine.

Lately I have been aware of certain symptoms of mental deterioration which I ascribed either to simple senility or watching weird movies on cable television. However, up until now I hadn't noticed any decline in my ability to think about sex. So I am not only chagrined but worried.

When you can't *think* about it anymore, it's time for Youth in Asia.

MATURITY COMES OF AGE

Goodbye, Pepsi Generation.

America's big advertisers, going with the population trend, have begun to aim their seductions at the "mature" and middle-aged rather than the very young, according to a recent newspaper account.

I have noticed several signs of this change, but I'm glad to know that it is not just an aberration, and that those who are no longer between two and twenty-four years of age can now find themselves in the ads and feel that they are actually a part of the circus.

Like most of my generation, I resented it for years when movies and television, the shows as well as the commercials, were pandering the youth's illusion that the young were the repository not only of all goodness and feeling, but also of all wisdom.

In many movies of the 1960s and 1970s, when the war babies had come into a bonanza of spending money and were old enough to protest and stay out all night, they were often represented as the entire population, and not simply the largest part of it.

Movies of the era might have given the impression to a visitor from space that this prosperous generation had sprung into being without parents, and that older people were simply a robot minority who could find employment only as policemen, teachers, judges, politicians and other authoritarian clowns.

Being thought incompetent by our children was no great penalty for having had them. Parents have always paid that price, and our children as parents will probably do the same. But it hurt when an industry whose executives and stockholders were of our own age so cruelly jilted us to court the young. Not only was advertising aimed at the Pepsi generation, but everything seemed to be made for it, too.

How helplessly we accepted their styles. I have a closet full of bell-bottom trousers, all of which I purchased under protest. I don't like bell-bottom trousers. I wore them when I was eleven years old because we all did, but later I joined the Marine Corps instead of the Navy, because you had to wear them in the Navy. Bell-bottom trousers look good only on flamenco dancers and little girls tap dancing in sailor suits.

Remember how the ads eulogized youthful possessiveness and macho arrogance? The low point was that beer commercial on TV in which a surly young punk, backed up by a pack of sneering friends, tried to intimidate an unseen appellant—you and me, by inference, since he was looking directly into the camera—by clutching his can of beer and snarling, "What! You want to take away my gusto!"

Now, according to the account in the paper, advertisers are aiming for what they are calling the "maturity market," a phrase that was held to be "surprisingly forthright," since maturity is regarded as "a close synonym for old."

I don't mind the phrase maturity market, being in some respects mature myself; but I'm not sure that phrase is so straightforward and synonymous with old. Even the youngest adults strive to appear "mature," and in fact aren't allowed to function as full citizens until they are legally certified as such. So the word is actually a Machiavellian equivocation. To the young, it is a flattering exaggeration, and to the old a flattering euphemism. But who can object? What a sensible world it would be if all of us were mature—no more, no less.

Not only are the advertisers raising their sights to catch the twenty-five-to-forty-four-year-olds, who have a lot of money and love to buy things. They are also zeroing in on the forty-five-to-sixty-four-year-olds, because their children are grown and gone and they have paid-for homes and money in the bank, and time on their hands. So it's not hard to see what the industry hopes to separate that age group from.

As glad as I will be to see more grown-ups on TV, I'll miss the old gang: those tawny girls playing volleyball, diving into sapphire pools, racing down snowy slopes, turning handsprings; those super boys on their endless holidays, celebrating the rites of manhood with their peers, catching passes, drinking Pepsi chug-a-lug, being good to their happy old mothers; those squeaky-haired McDonald's girls; those singing Continental stewardesses. It was a feast of health, joy, abundance, vigor, beauty, and everlasting youth.

But I will be glad to see the themes of our main art forms turn away from infants gumming oatmeal and adolescents giving each other sixty-four-tooth kisses, and onto chic gray-haired double-divorcées zipping to the liquor store in their Alfa Romeo Spyders to shop for liver paste and Chardonnay. Not that overnight we are going to see today's cupcake models replaced by clones of Lauren Bacall. But the trend is that way. Models used to be finished at twenty-five, we are told, but their average age today is 30. That does not seem old to me, but remember that not long ago the present "matures" thought of thirty as beyond the pale.

Unfortunately the change of focus has come too late for me to enjoy it to the full. They are aiming at the forty-five-to-sixty-four-year-old group just when I don't have a whole lot longer in it.

My only hope, I suppose, is to live until the Pepsi generation reaches sixty-four, and the advertisers come right out and aim for the "old market," because by then almost everybody will be old.

Of course by that time I will have moved on into senility and will be out of it again.

Needing some glue that would bond bricks to mortar, I went to the hardware store the other day and bought a tube of Wilhold, because I liked what it said about itself:

BONDS ANYTHING ANYWHERE ALMOST.

The ALMOST was in smaller letters than the rest of it, but it was there. It was modest, forthright, and refreshing, and though it was a very tiny mote in the sea of advertising that washes over us every day, I would like to think it signals a trend.

Of course saying that their glue would bond anything anywhere was laying it on a bit, and perhaps the Wilhold people added the "almost" to protect themselves against a charge of dishonest advertising.

I prefer to believe, though, that there was just a note of self-deprecating humor in it. They were spoofing, and the almost was their way of admitting it, to disarm nitpickers.

Such modesty is rare in advertising these days. Technology is our magic, and we have such faith in its miracles that most advertising is meant to imply that some "new, improved" soap or hair oil is the product of a technological "breakthrough." I always wonder how something called Super X and advertised for years as perfect could be new and improved every six months; but we will believe anything if it comes with a scientific pitch and has an X in it.

Cigarette advertising is the worst, since the theme of most brands is that they aren't as bad for you as the others. That is a negative approach but, in view of the facts, any other approach is hardly possible. Thus, we are urged to buy this cigarette or that because it has only 18.6 percent of something noxious in it compared with 19.7 percent in a competitive brand.

Beer ads, alas, have gone in the same direction, the current trend being toward so-called light beers, which allegedly won't make you as fat as the others.

It seems to me that advertising was more fun back in the 1920s, when it wasn't so inflated. The best cigarette ads ever turned out were those for Murads. "Be nonchalant," they suggested. "Light a Murad." This low-pressure admonition was always accompanied by an illustration in the style of John Held, Jr.—a sophisticated line drawing of some dapper young sheik dealing with an embarrassing moment by lighting a Murad.

One of these charmingly nonsensical ads, cut from an *American Mercury* of that era, has been sent to me by F. W. Audrain, and it is typical of the series.

In a sort of art deco line drawing by Rea Irvin, it shows a portly, well-dressed, bald-headed gentleman sitting in the lotus position on a Polynesian seashore. He has a lei around his neck and a flower on one ear and is being entertained by a hula dancer. A dreadnought of a woman who has just appeared on this scene under a dainty parasol is regarding the gentleman with ominous disapproval. The words are in light-face type, quiet and disarming:

LE MOMENT TERRIBLE (The Terrible Moment). If when traveling, you are surprised in a little pic-nic (pronounced peek-neek) by madame (the wife)... quelle affaire...be nonchalant...LIGHT A MURAD. Pronounced perfect by discriminating smokers.

Those ads were lighthearted trifles, but at the same time they showed more insight into the real reason people smoke cigarettes than all the less-tar, less-nicotine charts in vogue today. The reason most of us started smoking was that it gave us something to do with our hands. More than anything else in life, we wanted to be nonchalant.

Another company (was it Lucky Strike or Chesterfield?) had a long-run campaign in which a sweet young thing looked wistfully into the eyes of a young man who was smoking a cigarette and begged him, "Blow some my way." This campaign of course occurred at a time when ladies were not supposed to smoke, and those who did were considered naughty, if not depraved. It was an era to which Virginia Slims refers in its slogan, "You've come a long way, baby."

The same sort of low-key pitch was used by the Packard motor car company, which simply invited us to "Ask the man who owns one." I owned two Packards, though both were purchased second-hand, and if you ask me, they were wonderful.

Possibly such low-key spoofs wouldn't sell enough cigarettes in today's market, with the tar factor to consider; but the soft approach, either nonsensical or sentimental, has not been abandoned altogether.

Newspaper and magazine ads are expected to inform. Television ads have to entertain, or forget it. I am entertained by the television ad series in which James Garner and Mariette Hartley, as a married couple, engage in taut little cat-and-mouse games over the merits of the Polaroid camera. There is an erotic undercurrent in their terse exchanges, reminiscent of the provocative exchanges between William Powell and Myrna Loy as Nick and Nora Charles (who played in the days when eroticism had to be suggested, not displayed). Of course, the Garner-Hartley ads don't tell you much about Polaroid cameras, but they put you in a favorable mood to respond to the ads.

Speaking of great ads of the past, Rex E. Reed of Bakersfield recalls that he once met an "old gentleman" from New England who had been paid $100,000 for the famous BVD ad—"Next to myself I like BVDs best." He was worth it.

The pseudo-scientific tone of contemporary advertising is rooted in an old tradition. The claims made by manufacturers of headache tablets are only slightly refined from those made for Scott's emulsion in the December 1890 edition of the *Ladies Home Journal.*

"The disagreeable taste of cod liver oil is dissipated in Scott's emulsion of pure cod liver oil with hypophosphites of lime and soda. The patient suffering from consumption, bronchitis, cough, cold, or wasting diseases, may take the remedy with as much satisfaction as he would take milk. Physicians are prescribing it everywhere. It is a perfect emulsion, and a wonderful flesh producer."

Ladies reading that same issue were advised that Espey's fragrant cream "cures chapped hands, face, lips, or any roughness of the skin, prevents tendency to wrinkles or aging of skin, keeps the face and hands soft, smooth and plump. It is also highly recommended for applying and holding face powder. Once tried always used."

Also in that edition, a company named Bissell's advertised its product, a carpet sweeper "with latest improvements" as "The Most Popular Christmas Present in the World." Not even an "almost" would have mitigated that patent falsehood.

I suspect, though, that Wilhold is the only company in the history of American advertising that has modified its claim with the word almost, and I believe they can make it stick.

DIZZY DEAN

*"You learn 'em English,
I'll learn 'em baseball."*

In defending a certain idiomatic usage against the purists the other day I recalled our beloved baseball team, the Los Angeles Angels, and observed sadly that they had slud into oblivion.

I would have thought that the word slud, past tense of slide, was so well established in the American language that my using it would provoke no question.

I was surprised, therefore, on receiving two almost identical letters. One was from M. Puello of Sepulveda, and read in its entirety, as follows:

"Slud???"

The other was from Cathy Craig of Encino.

"Slud???
???"

I hope I have quoted Miss Craig correctly. I don't wish to deny her even one of the fifty-three question marks she evidently felt were required to express her puzzlement over the word slud.

—63—

Neither do I mean to make sport of M. Puello and Miss Craig for their ignorance of slud. All of us, no matter how broadly educated, have areas of ignorance which may astonish and dismay our friends. Nero Wolfe, the brilliant New York City detective, seems to know nothing of football or Bach.

Just as Wolfe doesn't know what a linebacker does for a living, my two correspondents evidently don't know that in baseball the past tense of *slide* is *slud*. Thus, it is said of a base runner who was required to hit the dirt and go in feet first for the bag, "He slud into third."

There's no need to reach for the dictionary. I've looked in Webster's unabridged, Random House and American Heritage and I must report, to the discredit of all three, that *slud* isn't there.

It has been said that a word previously disdained as slang or substandard can gain recognition as a good American word if it is used by a public figure who is considered exemplary in the American way of life. Thus, if Herbert Hoover, or even Harry Truman, had occasionally said "ain't" in their public utterances, the word ain't would have achieved the respectability so long sought for it by its champions.

Slud, however, was indeed given this respectability as a part of the regular vocabulary of one of the best loved Americans of the century, Dizzy Dean. Diz was born in Lucas, Arkansas, and dropped out of school in the second grade to help his ma and pa in the cotton fields. He is revered by baseball fans as one of the greatest pitchers who ever lived; but I personally think Dean's wit and his gift for language were a greater contribution to his country than the thirty games he won in 1934 with the Gas House Gang.

Dean often mixed grammar and wit to deal with sports writers who asked dumb questions. He rarely told the same story twice about his true name, age, and birthplace, and once when a writer asked him why he told such lies, Dean answered amiably: "Them ain't lies, them's scoops."

I hope my colleague Jim Murray won't care if I crib a few examples of what Murray calls the Dean's English. Most writers failed to get the inflection down just right in print, but Murray had a fine ear for it, as these samples from his column show:

"*Farn*—participle of the verb to fire, most often used as in 'Drysdale's really farn that ball today,' also as in 'light a far in the farplace.'

"*Karm*—verb meaning to bounce off of, usually spelled carom; usage restricted to line drives which 'karm off the wall.'

"*Airs*—miscues in the field, as in 'no runs, no hits, no airs.'"

I have stolen enough from Murray, I hope, to give the reader some idea of Dean's gift. Still, none of this may weigh much with M. Puello or Miss Craig, who evidently never heard Dean hold a room full of people spellbound with his description of a ballgame on radio or TV. Also, as I have conceded, the dictionaries apparently justify those question marks—all fifty-six of them—by omitting *slud*.

However, I wouldn't be surprised if this omission were to be corrected in the next editions. The lexicographers who compile these authoritative dictionaries are inclined to list any word that turns up in a responsible and influential context. Thus, I personally intend to send them the following editorial, which is reprinted here, in full, from the *Los Angeles Times* of July 20, 1974, the day Dizzy Dean was buried in Wiggins, Mississippi.

DIZZY DEAN
The game has slud back since he got out of it.

Yes, sir, I'm farn that off to the folks at Webster's today.

As promised, I have written to the big dictionary publishers suggesting that the word slud be included in their next editions, and now I am receiving just what they will want to see—public support.

"I propose," writes Peggy Walker of United Way, "that Webster's be petitioned to trade finalize and enthuse for slud, farn, karm and airs. They'd get four for two—and the English language would be enriched by the exchange."

"I'm with you," writes John M. Daley. "As you mentioned, usage of a slang or coined word by a prominent or famous person makes it a proper word. President Harding coined the word normalcy and President Roosevelt the word chiseler."

"I fully agree with you and the late Mr. Dean," writes John Thawley of Thousand Oaks, "that slud is a word. Diz was once taken to task by a schoolteacher for his constant use of the word ain't. His reply was classic. 'You learn 'em English and I'll learn 'em baseball.' "

John Kerr of Costa Mesa writes to say that slud is indeed in a dictionary, and enclosed a book called

How to Talk Pure Ozark in One Easy Lesson, by Dale Freeman of Springfield, Missouri. "Look on Page leb'm," says Kerr.

Yep, it is there on Page leb'm. "*SLUD*—He slud into what he thought was second base." This handy little book also includes such words as *rang* ("when they got married he put a rang on her finger"); *rawzum* ("he put a little rawzum on the bow of his fiddle")' and *retch* ("Clyde retch out and grub her around the waist").

Betty Scudder of Altadena writes that her daughter recently returned from a visit to Texas with a dictionary listing *are,* meaning sixty minutes ("I'll meet you in a are"); *grain,* a color ("he's just grain with envy"); and *toad,* past tense of tell ("Ah toad yew never to do thet").

But I don't mean to ask too much of the dictionary people all at once. This time round, I'll settle for *slud.*

I am especially pleased, by the way, to hear again from Cathy Craig of Encino, who set off this whole movement by questioning my use of slud with her laconic note. I'm afraid that in exposing this tiny bit of ignorance I subjected Miss Craig to some embarrassment.

"I feel I must apologize," Miss Craig writes now, "for the thoughts I was entertaining the last time I wrote to you. I jumped to the erroneous conclusion that you were using a grammatically incorrect past tense of the verb to slide. To be sure, you were; however, I was unaware of the acceptable idiomatic usage of the word slud.

"Believe me, I have been corrected. My mother was horrified that she and my father could have possibly neglected such an important area of my education as

Dizzy Dean (she woke me up this morning to tell me). My only excuse is my age. I was very young when Dizzy Dean was busy rewriting the English language...."

That is a candid and charming letter. Miss Craig needn't apologize or feel bad. She isn't the only one who doesn't know everything, as I am reminded by a letter from C.F.V., who asks me to use his initials only. He writes:

"Re your statement, 'All of us, no matter how broadly educated, have areas of ignorance....' I would suggest that you substitute nescience for ignorance.

"Ignorance is not knowing something which you should know; nescience is not knowing something which you could not reasonably be expected to know."

Frankly, I didn't know that.

Meanwhile, I have received an answer from G. & C. Merriam Co., publishers of the Merriam-Webster dictionaries, explaining why they have not listed *slud* in their dictionaries.

The meat of it is in this sentence: "*Slud* is virtually unknown outside of references to Dizzy Dean, and continued references to his use of it, as your 'salute,' only emphasize the peculiarity of the usage rather than spread it."

That sentence fascinates me because I believe "as your salute" should have been "like your salute," and I suspect that the author of it, like so many fastidious writers, had been frightened by the abuse heaped by purists on the "Winstons taste good like a cigarette should" ad, and had mistakenly inferred from this furor that *like* should always be *as*.

It seemed to me that a lexicographer who would write *as* when he should have written *like* is in no position to criticize a word like *slud*, but I appreciate his courtesy in answering my letter, and I doubt that old Diz would give a hoot, or even a holler.

HOW IS THE PATIENT?

"As well as can be expected."

Some people have eyes that are oversensitive to light and they must wear sunglasses even on cloudy days; others suffer from too much noise, or smoke; but the forgotten victim of our modern environment is the person who happens to be extremely sensitive to illogical or ambiguous signs, bulletins and messages, and for him there is no remedy.

"This morning," writes Noel Temple of Beaumont, who seems to have this problem, "I read in my newspaper where a man was shot. A few hours later, he was reported to be in 'very satisfactory condition.' It causes me to wonder if he is in better condition than before he was shot, and if that is the case, I wonder why he wasn't shot sooner, or at least a couple of more times."

I sympathize with Temple. Many times, as a news writer, I was required to telephone hospitals for a report on the condition of some person who had recently suffered what the layman might think of as an unsatisfactory accident, such as being shot, only to be told that the patient was "in satisfactory condition."

Invariably I would then ask what exactly was meant by "satisfactory," knowing that the person had been shot three times and thrown from a moving train, only to be told that for further information I would have to talk with the doctor, who was of course unavailable.

Actually, "satisfactory condition" was a substitute for the previous all-purpose hospital phrase, which was that the patient was "doing as well as can be expected." Like "satisfactory," this phrase always had a momentarily reassuring effect, until one had thanked the hospital and hung up and begun to think about it. As well as he could be expected by whom? By his wife? His mother? His insurance company? Under scrutiny it wasn't a very satisfactory answer.

It is odd, though, that Temple should have come upon "satisfactory condition" in a recent newspaper, because I have noticed that this phrase also has been replaced, just as it replaced "as well as can be expected." The phrase in current use is "in guarded condition." Every day we read that someone is "in guarded condition."

Whether a patient in guarded condition is worse off than a patient in satisfactory condition or one who is doing as well as can be expected, I don't know. It seems to me, though, that any patient in a hospital ought to be in guarded condition, or what is he doing in a hospital, at the rates he must be paying? For that kind of money a person ought to be guarded, at least.

I suspect that "guarded" doesn't mean anything essentially different from "satisfactory" or "as well as can be expected," but is simply a new placebo thought up by hospitals after the public had caught on to the old ones, and like its predecessors it means merely that the patient is not dead and that the hospital actually doesn't know how he is, because life is uncertain at best, and they want to cover all the bases.

That isn't the only one that bothers Temple. "The other day," he goes on," I heard a California Highway Patrolman, speaking on TV, make the statement, 'There are too many traffic fatalities.' He didn't say what the right amount of traffic fatalities should be. If one is not given a set of numbers to shoot for, there is no way to know when to stop the fatalities."

Even within his own family, Temple is not safe from the illogical, the meaningless or the ambiguous: "My own father has a notation by his phone which says, 'For the correct time call 853-1212.' My father won't answer me when I ask who to call for the incorrect time."

He might have hoped for surcease in the Canadian mountains. But there, beside a tranquil lake, he found this: "It is illegal to tie a boat up for a long period of time." His equanimity dissolved, and evidently he spent the day brooding about that sign. What exactly was a "long period of time"?

"Now I submit," he says, "that what might be a short time to a man awaiting execution might be an exceedingly long time to a man who knew his wife was out with another man."

He is right. "A long period of time" is an indefinite term, beyond measuring, and it depends on who is doing what to whom. What is satisfactory to the doctor may not be so to the patient. If there can be too many traffic fatalities, then theoretically there can be too few. If there is a correct time there must be an incorrect time, but who keeps it?

The most a logical man can hope for in such a world, I suppose, is to go on doing as well as can be expected.

I am happy to say that I have now received some clarification of hospital talk from the medical profession itself.

While I would not classify this clarification as quite satisfactory, at least it is fairly good, and perhaps as good as could be expected.

I may not have been far off the mark, it appears, when I guessed that each of these ratings means merely that the patient is not dead and that the hospital doesn't know how he is.

"I think you are correct," writes Dr. John S. Marsh, a Whittier neurosurgeon, "in your surmise that there is an element of cover-up going on. A report of how a patient is will be taken to imply how he is going to be, which no one knows for sure, especially the hospital spokesman. 'Guarded' really refers to the hospital's desire not to be made to look foolish if a patient does better or worse than expected.

"Once when I asked a patient how he felt," Dr. Marsh recalls, "he said, 'I'm in good shape for the shape I'm in,' and we both knew what he meant, but it would have been hard to tell that to a third party."

From Janice F. Atzen, information director of Long Beach Community Hospital, I have received a copy of the California Hospital Association News Code, which specifies terms to be used in reports to outsiders on a patient's condition:

Good—Vital signs are stable and within normal limits. Patient is conscious and comfortable. Indicators are excellent.

Fair—Vital signs are stable and within normal limits. Patient is conscious but may be uncomfortable. Indicators are favorable.

Serious—Vital signs may be unstable and not within normal limits. Patient is acutely ill. Indicators are questionable.

Critical—Vital signs are unstable and not within normal limits. Patient may be unconscious. Indications are unfavorable.

Dr. Marsh also acknowledges this standardized declension, but points out: "This is more meaningful to third parties if they know the comparators, as 'good' is indeed a relative matter."

There is another scale of terms, he adds, to express the degree of "diagnostic certainty" felt by the physician. "If I feel secure in a diagnosis, I will say the diagnosis is, for instance, 'brain tumor,' but if I'm a little less sure I say 'probably brain tumor.' 'Possible brain tumor' fits just above 'rule out brain tumor.'

"But the Joint Commission on Accreditation of Hospitals will not accept a chart diagnosis of 'probably' and Medicare will not reimburse a patient for the expense of a computerized brain scan if 'rule out' is on the diagnosis. Oddly, both will accept 'headache,' which is not really a diagnosis at all but a symptom.

"Was it the Walrus," Dr. Marsh asks "who told Alice a word meant precisely what he intended it to mean, and the question was who was to be the master?" (No, Dr. Marsh, I would rule out the Walrus. Possibly it was Humpty Dumpty.)

Meanwhile an attorney, Charles P. McKenney, notes an ominous medical phenomenon: "Your recent article about phrases and expressions used by the press reminded me," he writes, "that no one is taking seriously the No. 1 reported killer today—the apparent heart attack. Several of these are reported each day, yet no one seems concerned enough to hold a celebrity tennis tournament to help stamp out this apparently serious killer."

I'm glad McKenney brought that up. I have long been worried by the rising incidence of fatal apparent heart attacks. My guess, though, is that doctors and hospitals are not to blame for this epidemic, so much as newspapers. I would have thought apparent heart attacks wouldn't be fatal; but as McKenney points out, they are the No. 1 killer, at least among persons whose deaths are thought worthy of notice by the press.

Occasionally some reporter, evidently suspecting that an apparent heart attack shouldn't be fatal, will write instead that a person "apparently died of a heart attack." Of course that does not leave us wondering whether the person died of a real heart attack or only an apparent heart attack so much as it leaves us wondering whether he died at all, or only apparently died.

It is a great irony, I think, that newspaper writers who so callously note the passing of their fellow citizens in apparent heart attacks apparently are immune to the disease themselves.

Most of us, I'm afraid, are doomed to die, apparently, of a ruptured syntax.

GOOD MORNING

"Not this morning."

"How long has it been," my wife asked me recently, "since we've said 'Good morning' to each other?"

A simple enough question, perhaps, but somehow I found it ominous. There was an insidious curve in it, like the classic question that implies guilt and permits only an answer that seems to admit it: "When did you stop beating your wife?"

The question assumed that my wife and I at one time had customarily said "Good morning" to each other, presumably on first arising in the morning, but that somewhere along the line we had stopped. While the accusation was not explicit, I had no doubt that if we had stopped, it was my fault.

"Did we ever?" I said at last, after thinking about it a minute.

"Did we ever what?"

"Say, 'Good morning.' You just asked me how long it had been since we stopped."

"Well, how long has it been?"

"What I have to know first," I pointed out, "is whether we ever said 'Good morning.'"

"Well, we must have. People do."

"What you mean, then," I said, "is that somewhere in the past, a long time ago, we had a habit of saying 'Good morning' to each other to begin the day."

"Something like that."

"Well, then, no. I don't believe we ever said 'Good morning' as a routine thing. Maybe now and then on an especially good morning, on a weekend in Palm Springs or something like that, but not as a daily ritual. People only do that in Agatha Christie, before they know there's another dead body in the garden."

"I think it would have been nice," she said.

She sounded disappointed, as though it was something that would have made her happier and cost me nothing but a couple of easily spoken words. I began to feel guilty, which is exactly what I knew I was going to wind up feeling when she asked me the question in the first place.

Maybe such marital routines are useful at that, I thought. Their main function is to get a couple through a difficult passage, to ease a rude encounter when both of them are in an uncertain temper, and any spontaneous conversation flowing directly from that touchy situation is not to be trusted.

Thus, in saying "Good morning," each person acknowledges the physical presence and rights of the other, and signals, without saying so specifically, that further conversation is to be avoided until after the paper has been brought in and the coffee has dripped.

On the contrary, I feel it is safer to say nothing at all until the paper is in and the coffee has dripped.

Those conditions are a minimum for the beginning of a day's verbal exchanges between husband and wife—or any roommates, whatever their legal status. That is why, at our house, after the clock radio goes on, so much time passes before one or the other of us gets up. We have no rules about who gets up first, so this is settled every day by a contest of wills. Sooner or later one simply knows that the other is not going to give in; so the loser gets up and makes the coffee and brings the paper in.

Whichever spouse outwaits the other does not then get up, of course, until he or she hears the front door open and close, knowing the paper is in, and calculates that there has been sufficient time for the coffee to drip. A premature move in this situation is disastrous. Then you have two people lurching about the kitchen, at least one of them in his bare feet (since I can never find my slippers and probably don't have any), before the paper is in and the coffee is made. It is hard enough simply trying not to bump into one another, and any attempt at civilized badinage is hopeless.

We ran into an impasse the other morning, a day or two after the question came up about saying "Good morning." We were both about to get a late start on the day, so we had to give up outwaiting the other in bed, and got up at the same time.

Without discussing it, we automatically chose our chores. Since it was raining, I made the coffee and my wife went out to get the paper, which would have been foolish for me, without my slippers.

When she came in neither of us said anything for a while. It just seemed wiser not to. Then I remembered her question. I thought it might be interesting to give it a try.

"Good morning," I said.

"Not this morning," she said.

That's probably what happened. We used to say "Good morning" but I tried it once on a rainy day when she had to go out for the paper, and it didn't seem worth the risk after that.

I may try it again, though, as soon as the storm is over.

It was no surprise to me to read in our paper the other day that a large number of cohabiting couples in California are married and don't think it's half bad. I'm sure the statistics will disappoint the experts who have been warning for years that California is Sodom on wheels and that sooner or later God will destroy us all in a thunderclap or more probably an earthquake.

But I have never doubted that marriage, or monogamous cohabitation without a marriage ceremony, would remain popular despite the tempting alternatives, if only because it takes a long time for mates to learn how to communicate without talking in full sentences.

Anyone who is single, or can remember being single, knows that the most trying aspect of one-on-one relationships in their nascent stage is the necessity of having to explain oneself, one's background, one's likes and dislikes.

Unless a couple have grown up together and been childhood sweethearts, they have to learn all there is to know about each other in order to speak each other's language. In the beginning, the young man hasn't the slightest idea what the young woman is talking about when she says, for example, "I'd like to see that movie with what's-his-name in it."

" 'What movie?" he is obliged to ask. And she

replies, "You know. It has the man who played in the other one."

"What other one?"

"The one with what's-her-name in it."

"I don't know what you're talking about."

Now that kind of an exchange is tiring and frustrating, and in no time at all a couple caught up in its toils will become quite impatient with one another.

Couples who are virtually strangers are always obliged to talk autobiographically, to throw out bits of personal history, to declare such idiosyncrasies as a taste for rabbit; to explain who Uncle Fred is, and why one can't read Norman Mailer but loves Woody Allen, or vice versa.

These self-revealing and exploratory conversations take time, and in fact some couples never finish with them, so that after fifteen years of marriage the wife may be quite surprised to learn that her husband can't stand oregano.

The main reason for prolonged monogamy, it seems to me, is that someday, finally, a couple emerge into a state of perfect knowledge and understanding of one another, like that lovely photograph by Eugene Smith of the two little children walking out of the woods and into the sunlight, hand in hand.

What makes courtship and early marriage so difficult is the conversation that unfamiliarity demands. In the beginning, when boy meets girl, he presumably knows nothing about her that his eyes can't tell him, and vice versa. Thereupon, if there is any mutual attraction, they begin that cautious dialogue of interrogation, revelation and dissimulation that is never utterly candid, and which will still be in progress eighteen years later, when the children begin to leave the nest.

It is at this point that the husband may say, "Now what were you saying?" And the wife says, "I was saying I have never really cared for housework." And the husband says, "I didn't know that. I don't like yard work, either."

And from that point on they begin to understand each other.

Couples who have lived long together are able to communicate with a minimum of exposition, depending instead on code words and phrases that are ostensibly free of information, but nonetheless are clearly comprehended.

My wife and I have reached that enlightened stage, and while we can still carry on a fairly intelligible conversation in the presence of others, our private exchanges are conducted in a form of shorthand, like the following:

"What's on the cable?"

"I don't know."

"Isn't it one you wanted to see?"

"With what's-his-name?"

"No, the one what's-her-name's married to."

"You don't like him."

"No, I don't like her."

"She isn't in it, is she?"

"In what?"

"The other one."

"Oh, no."

As what's-his-name said, "Marriage begins as a play and ends as a game of chess."

Manfred Wolf, a professor of English at San Francisco State College, has been listening carefully to conversation and believes that it's a declining if not a lost art.

In an article published by the *San Francisco Examiner,* the professor identified a number of styles and gambits that he finds especially irritating, among them the practice of beginning a conversation *in medias res,* i.e., in the middle of things.

"Homer's epics opened this way," he points out, "and the audience was supposed to gather—from the unfolding of the talk and from a later recounting of earlier events—how it had all come to this point."

I believe Professor Wolf means the kind of conversation that begins, to use my own example, "Melba's walked out on Fred again, but I think it's Charlotte's fault, ever since Roger came into the picture."

Wolf doesn't say whether he's married or not, but it's pretty obvious that he isn't. Almost every conversation between a man and a woman who have been married for a long time begins *in medias res.* For example, if my wife were to say, "Melba's walked out on Fred again, but I think it's Charlotte's fault, ever since Roger came into the picture," I would know exactly what she meant, and would say "I always thought Irma was the snake in the grass."

Now to Professor Wolf that might not make sense. But it not only would make sense to my wife and me, it is in fact a rather artful bit of dialogue. Anyone who was familiar with the affairs of Melba, Fred, Charlotte and Irma would have to admire the way we had summed up the current situation in hardly more than two dozen words. Furthermore, critical analysis would show that it had insight, clarity, and a remarkable economy of expression; in short, it was conversation of the first water.

Professor Wolf also observes that people talk "right past each other," each pursuing a separate line of thought, with a result that he likens to the Theater of the Absurd. For example, he cites the following exchanges:

> HIMSELF: I was in Mexico last summer.
> THE OTHER PARTY: We were in Mexico three years ago, and we loved it. we . . .

> HIMSELF: I just got out of the hospital.
> THE OTHER PARTY: I was in last March, and it was no picnic. . . .

I am rather surprised that Professor Wolf would consider these two bits of dialogue examples of the decline of conversation. The truth is, they are examples of very artful conversation indeed.

One of the arts of conversation is to checkmate the other party before he gets up too much steam and momentum. What this requires is the quick block, or parry. Every opening gambit has within it the seed of its own destruction. The alert conversationalist, cornered by another party who has recently been to Mexico, is in an advantageous position if he himself has been to Mexico more recently. He can check the other party at once with the news that everything there has changed depressingly, and he doesn't really want to hear how it was when the other party was there.

On the other hand, if he has not been to Mexico more recently than the other party, he may still seize the advantage by interrupting to say that he was in Mexico long before the other party. It was so wonderful then and has changed so much, for the worse, that he doesn't want to hear about it.

Even better, if the other party says he has been to Mexico, while he himself has been to Yemen, Togo, Guinea-Bissau or some even more remote and exotic place, there is no need to let the fellow who has only been to Mexico finish a sentence.

As for Professor Wolf's other example, any person who starts a conversation by saying he just got out of the hospital is pitifully inexperienced, especially if he is talking to anyone over forty-five years old.

We had three couples over for dinner last Sunday night, and three of us had recently had operations. Naturally, the one who had had the most recent operation had the advantage, but even before he could get to his anesthetic one of the others, who happened to be a lady, pulled up her blouse and showed her abdominal scar.

That is the sort of thing one couldn't have done at a proper dinner party before the Johnson administration, and if Professor Wolf is interested in fixing the exact time that conversation in America started to decline, I believe he might find that it was back there when President Johnson had his gall bladder out. There is no use blaming television for everything.

But I share Professor Wolf's concern. Good conversation is one of the skills that separate us from the brutes, and its decline would certainly signal the decline of civilization.

I intend to do what I can to keep it alive, and with my recent operation, my recent trip to Mexico, and my recent grandson, I ought to have a great year.

YOU COULD LOOK IT UP

"Family:
A thing you live with."

I have a letter from a man in Florida who said he had read something of mine in a Florida newspaper and was irritated on finding a word he didn't know. He said he was no longer young enough to look up words, even if he had a dictionary, which he didn't, and he wished I would quit using strange ones.

I give serious thought to every complaint, hoping always for improvement, but it is impossible to know what the limits of any one person's vocabulary may be, not to mention those of the generality, if you will forgive an apophasis.

My policy, therefore, has always been to use the word that best says what I am trying to say, not that I can always think of it; and I am happy if it happens to be a short and common word, one with a good chance of being understood, but if not, so be it. I use the word that means what I want to say, and hope for the best. Readers who don't know the word may entertain themselves by looking it up, or by making an inference of its meaning from the context (a risky business), or skip it, or turn the page, or dash off an angry letter telling me to quit using sesquipedalianisms.

My answer to the man in Florida, by the way, was that if he thought *I* used big words he should try reading William F. Buckley, who likes to take quantum leaps beyond sesquipedalianisms, which are merely very long words, to hippopotomonstrosesquipedalianisms, which are very, very long words.

I usually read Mr. Buckley with pleasure, though I sometimes think he deliberately uses words that I don't know just to irritate me personally; which is of course like thinking that God is aware of your particular existence and does things just to irritate you personally. I always look up Buckley's words, a practice which, over the years, has not only enlarged my vocabulary and my understanding, but also enriched my life.

I of course suggested to the man in Florida that he might also enjoy such rewards if he were to buy a good dictionary and learn a word or two every day. But one doesn't have to own a dictionary to enjoy reading or even to write well. Shakespeare didn't own an English dictionary because there weren't any. When the erudite Dr. Samuel Johnson compiled his dictionary in the eighteenth century, he said it was meant for "the use of such as aspire to exactness of criticism or elegance of style," noting that such a book was not generally considered necessary to "the greater number of readers, who, seldom intending to write or presuming to judge, turn over books only to amuse their leisure, and to gain degrees of knowledge suitable to lower characters, or necessary to the common business of life...."

That is rather an elitist attitude, and one that should not apply in times like ours, when words are printed or broadcast daily by the millions for the millions, often with ambiguous results, and when reliable dictionaries are plentiful and cheap.

Just the other day a reader named Bartlett Rackliffe took the trouble to send me a word he had "discovered" in a dictionary. It was *mumpsimus:* "an error or prejudice obstinately clung to; the term is supposedly taken from the story of an illiterate priest who, in his devotions, had for thirty years used *mumpsimus* for the proper Latin word *sumpsimus,* and who, on his mistake being pointed out to him, replied, 'I will not change my mumpsimus for your new sumpsimus.'"

I don't know whether I will ever have a chance to use that word again, but at least I know about it, and if you know the word *mumpsimus,* it makes you more aware that mumpsimuses exist, and you are more likely to find one in your own pocket, and knowing it for what it is, throw it out.

Recently Dr. Willard E. Goodwin of the UCLA School of Medicine sent me *comether* (pronounced *ku-meth'-er*), a noun of Irish origin which is simply a variant of the noun *come-hither,* meaning: "an enticing invitation; winning talk or ways; (she could put the come-hither on any man)."

In its full form, come-hither, the word is widely used as an adjective, as in "she gave him her come-hither look," and few of us have been so unlucky as not to have felt ourselves the object of one. It is interesting to note, therefore, that in the beginning come-hither was "a call to animals," including pigs, I presume. This suggests that when a woman gives a man a come-hither look she is simply appealing to the beast in him.

Meanwhile, on my own, while reading William Manchester's memoir of his years as a Marine Corps rifleman in World War II, *Goodbye, Darkness,* I came upon *quiddity,* which I didn't seem to know, and found out that it comes from the Latin *quid* (what, something, anything) and means: "the real nature of a thing: essence."

There are ways, of course, of looking up improbable and wonderful words without going through a standard dictionary, thus not having to waste time on 50,000 words you already know. One of these shortcuts is *Mrs. Byrne's Dictionary of Unusual, Obscure, and Preposterous Words,* by Josefa Heifetz Byrne (University Books, 1974).

To those adjectives Mrs. Byrne might have added outrageous, neglected, comical, repulsive, useless and sesquipedalian words; and then some.

The book has only 237 pages but it can be read without a magnifying glass by almost anyone outside a gerontocomium and is certainly indispensable for anyone who didn't know, for example, that *exsibilate* means to reject something with a hissing sound.

As I thumbed through it, looking for a clue to Mrs. Byrne's criteria for deciding which words to include, it dawned on me that she didn't have any, except her own caprice. She must have gone through all the other dictionaries like a little girl picking wildflowers.

On the first page we find *abbey-lubber,* defined by Mrs. Byrne as "a lazy monk pretending to be ascetic; any loafer." This definition, by the way, is typical of Mrs. Byrne. She does not fozzle; neither does she twaddleize. She is short, sharp and graphic as a penpoint.

She is fascinated, as I am, by the words for self-righteous morality and its exponents. We find the word *antithalian,* which means "against pleasure." She skips *bowdlerize* and *comstockery,* but includes my own favorite, *wowser,* which she neatly defines as "a pecksniffian puritan." *Pecksniffian,* by the way, Mrs. Byrne defines as "hypocritical, insincere and gutless."

Inevitably she includes a good many words that at first glance seem obsolete. For example, *stylite,* meaning "ascetics who lived on top of pillars; also called pillarists." Ascetics no longer live on top of pillars, as far as I know, but it occurs to me that the word might well be revived to apply to us abbey-lubbers who live on top of newspaper columns.

She includes words for things that everyone does but no one knows the word for. For example, *apophasis.* That means "mentioning something by saying it won't be mentioned: 'We won't mention his filthy habits.'" Also we find *asteism,* "an ingeniously polite insult," which is also an art whose most skilled practitioners are ignorant of its name.

There are forgotten words I would like to see back in harness, like *giffgaff,* meaning "give and take, informal conversation." Also, *mingy,* meaning "mean and stingy." And words that might as well stay dead and buried. *Tyromancy,* for example, which means "fortune telling by watching cheese coagulate."

In a very subtle way Mrs. Byrne expresses her feminism by using *she* or *her* in her definitions, instead of *he* and *him*. She defines *frotteur,* for example, as "someone who gets her kicks by rubbing against people in crowds" (which certainly seems unladylike). I might not have noticed it in that case, but later she defines *postliminium* as "when a war prisoner returns to her own country," and that gives her little game away. Of course she may have been thinking of Helen of Troy.

Mrs. Byrne gives us words for the most loathsome diseases and manias, and the whole range of human ugliness and folly. She also gives us such palatable words as *fimblefamble,* meaning "an excuse, particularly a phony one," *gracile*—"graceful and slender," and *euphelicia*—"healthiness resulting from having all one's wishes granted."

I also found *loganamnosis*—"a mania for trying to recall forgotten words," *logastellus*—"a person whose enthusiasm for words outstrips his knowledge of them," and *lopadotemachoselachogaleokranioleipsanodrimphypotrimmatosilophiopar amelitokatakechmenokichlepilossyphophattoperisteralektryonoptekphalliokigklopeleiolagoiosiraiobaphetraganopterygon*—"a goulash composed of the leftovers from the meals of the leftovers from the meals of the last two weeks."

To paraphrase the little girl in the *New Yorker* cartoon, I say it's hash, and the hell with it.

Among the obvious gifts that my family was unable to give me for Father's Day was a dictionary. I prize dictionaries the way some people prize orchids or goldfish, but I now have all I can handle, especially with the acquisition of Mrs. Byrne's.

I might profit, however, from one of the dictionaries put together by the pupils out at the Sherman Oaks Presbyterian Nursery School, as gifts for their fathers on Father's Day. One of the teachers, Mary DiMaggio, teaches her pupils how to use dictionaries. "We discuss what a dictionary is," she explains, "the children give me words, and we look them up."

Then Mrs. DiMaggio gives the children words and asks them to define them. "For the most part I try to use words they're familiar with or at least may have heard. Even if a youngster doesn't know the word, he'll usually bluff it out."

Naturally, children's definitions are likely to be cute. But sometimes they glow with insights into the adult world, and at the worst they suggest how really hard it is to define anything at all.

Anyone who thinks it's easy might try defining the word *embarrassing*, for instance. Or a simple word like *chair*. I doubt if most of us can do much better than these examples from Mrs. DiMaggio's four- and five-year-olds.

Embarrassing—when you're undressed and somebody's almost there. . . . When somebody loves you. . . . You do something wrong at a party.
Cheap—It's like when you're a millionaire. . . . A bird. . . . You don't have to give the store man all your money. . . . It goes baa.
Accident—Whenever you did something that your mother doesn't like what you did.
Analogy—You sneeze and stuff.

Attack—A thing you hang on.

Blunder—It makes your house wet.

Extinct—When something's not working.

Friend—A girl or a boyfriend and when you get near them you do stuff.

Fossil—It makes hot water come out of it.... The wet sand and something on top of it like a dead fish or a dead man it turns into a fossil when it dries up and the man doesn't even know it.

Florist—Puts the floor on.

Family—A thing that you live with.... Where animals and people live together.

Fun—Is walking up a slide in tennis shoes.

Germ—Like someone breathes at you.

Moisture—My sister found a moisture and she found a pearl in it.

Nature—God takes care of all things.

Pharmacist—Someone who works at a store with apples and fruit.

Problem—Someone wants you to do what you don't want to do.

Trouble—When you get into your father's grease.... You go to your room and stay for a year.... It rains and you can't go out and your sister can.

Terminate—Someone comes and sprays around your house.

Secret—Only letting yourself know.

Surprise—You can't wait and you don't know what it is but you want it.

Ridiculous—All the people at the hotel where we went on vacation.

From the results of these early encounters with the lures, illusions and pitfalls of the English language, we get a glimpse into a strange and wonderfully distorted children's world.

It would be a world full of dangers, like when you stepped on an attack or somebody breathed at you or the bug man came to terminate the house. It would be a world of joys, like when father came home from the pharmacist's with apples or you found a pearl in the moisture. And it would be a happy world in a house where people and animals lived together, and there would be no reason to worry about the TV going extinct or getting into your father's grease, because God takes care of all things.

Anyway, the children's definitions certainly make more sense than "Love means never having to say you're sorry."

PORT OUT, STARBOARD HOME

Is POSH only a pretty myth?

Recently I had a letter from Harold R. Lichterman, a lawyer, wondering if I knew the origin of the word *posh,* meaning elegant or luxurious, and adding that he had written the publishers of the *Oxford English Dictionary,* asking if they knew.

He referred to the popular belief that posh comes from the term Port Out, Starbord Home, in reference to the shady thus more expensive steamship accommodations on voyages between England and India in the days before air conditioning; but he wasn't convinced of its authenticity.

I couldn't help him, except to say that I too was familiar with the Port Out, Starboard Home story, but even though it was charming and plausible, I had often heard it debunked as a pretty myth.

So I awaited with as much excitement as he did an answer from the august publishers of the *Oxford English Dictionary;* not that I was sure he would receive one. I remembered my own disappointing experience in writing the three foremost American dictionaries to ask why none of them listed Dizzy Dean's word *slud*. But I should have kept in mind the British respect for scholarship, and for the dogged tenacity of the *Oxford English Dictionary*'s etymologists in pursuit of the tiniest and most elusive clues. No hare is too swift for their hounds to follow, no trail too cold for their noses, no trophy too trifling to rouse their ardor. Also, they are terribly courteous.

Lichterman has now received the OED's answer, and kindly sent me a copy, which I quote in part:

"Thank you for your letter of 8 March concerning the origin of the word *posh*. The view that the word is an acronym of Port Out, Starboard Home is a commonly held one, but it had not attained the current popularity when the 1933 Supplement to the *Oxford English Dictionary* was compiled.

"One of the earliest occurrences in print of this suggestion known to us is in the *London Times Literary Supplement* for 17 October, 1935. Exhaustive research has failed to produce evidence of substance in support of this claim, and there are strong arguments in favour of regarding it as a 'folk' etymology. You may be interested to read an elaborate treatment of this evidence in an article by G. Chowdharay-Best in *The Mariner's Mirror*, January 1971 (photocopy enclosed).

"Our evidence for the word *posh* in print still supports the etymology suggested in the 1933 Supplement and a connection with the use of the word meaning 'a dandy,' which dates from the latter part of the nineteenth century, remains probable. We shall be presenting this evidence in detail when we deal with the word *posh* in the revised Supplement in due course." (Signed, R. S. Allen, assistant editor, general.)

G. Chowdharay-Best's treatment of the question runs two pages, single-spaced in small type, and is illuminated by numerous bits of evidence on both sides of the Port Out, Starboard Home theory.

At the outset he disposes of the argument that *posh* could not have derived from Port Out, Starboard Home because in the nineteenth century the word *larboard* was in use, instead of *port*, and so the acronym would have been *losh*.

"With respect," Chowdharay-Best observes, "I do not think this particular objection can be sustained, for the large *Oxford Dictionary* (vol. VII (1935), p. 1137, col. 3) cites under 'port' an Admiralty Order of 22 Nov., 1844 directing the discontinuance of the use of the word 'larboard' and the quotations show that port in this sense was used as long ago as 1625-44...."

But after holding against that assault, the theory fades.

Having been a frequent traveler to India in the heyday of steam, Chowdharay-Best confesses a "sneaking sympathy" with the popular derivation. But his exhaustive search into literature, travelers' diaries, and records dating back to 1842, when the Peninsular & Oriental Steam Navigation Company began running ships through the Red Sea, failed to uncover persuasive evidence to support it.

Finally, his study of deck plans and other arrangements shows that the term Port Out, Starboard Home for the most expensive suites and cabins would have made no sense. Alas.

But I certainly have to throw in with people who care that much about a frivolous word, and who feel constrained to give such responsible and elaborate attention to an idle query from a stranger living among the illiterate colonials a sea and a continent from London.

H. L. Mencken, when asked what book he would want to have with him if he were marooned on a desert island, unhesitatingly said the *Oxford English Dictionary*.

That's good enough for me. I just hope it's good enough for Suzanne Pleshette. But we'll have to wait for the revised Supplement, of course.

In challenging the popular myth about the origin of *posh* I seem to have disenchanted some readers, who didn't really want to be disenchanted, but left others quite unshaken in their faith. It may seem much ado about nothing, to be sure, but legends do not pass, especially pretty ones, without mourners.

"You have just shot down posh, my most effective conversation electrifier," writes Roger Johnson of Lake Havasu City. "It will be sorely missed. For example: You walk into a party, all strangers, and after a brittle silence someone says to the host, 'Wilbur, you've certainly got a posh apartment.' Suddenly you are at ease. 'Interesting word, posh. Dates back to pukka sahib travel between London and India. Everyone wanted to go out and come back on the shady side. If you had clout as well as money you could buy a ticket that said Portside Out, Starboard Home, which kept you relatively cool for the round trip while the cloutless perspired on the wrong side of the boat.' Silence and ill-concealed admiration. 'So *that's* where posh comes from,' says the mysterious, beautiful guest of honor. 'Well, I never.' "

Jack Taylor of Burbank recalls a romantic incident in support of the myth: "In 1927, while serving aboard *HMS Iron Duke* in quite the lowest form of life afloat—boy 1st class—we were tied up to the Mole of Gibraltar, and a large P. & O. liner entered harbor and tied up to a more prestigious jetty. That night, in the soft moonlight, the liner was ablaze with varicolored lights and the passengers were whooping it up to "The Blue Danube" and "Oh, Miss Hannah." I was on the foc'sle, entranced by this high-class living, when an AB alongside me said, 'No wonder it is called posh,' and when I asked him what he meant, he replied, 'Well, Peninsular & Oriental Shipping Co. was too big for Lloyds of London's board, so they shortened it to POSH, and as it carried only rajahs, tea planters and rich colonials, it soon became synonymous with the well-to-do.' "

Sic transit posh.

WORKOHOLIC? APPALLING!

"We might as well preach against sin."

In a letter to the editor of the *Los Angeles Times* a subscriber named Green exercised her rights by protesting a surname I had used. I had been discussing the problem of how to begin a business letter when Dear Sir or Gentlemen might not be appropriate, and to illustrate the point I used a hypothetical law firm, one of whose members was a Ms. Meddlesome. (At least that's the way it came out in type.)

Mrs. Green's comment was exemplary in its brevity, and deserves to be reprinted: "After reading the fine article on women and the law," she wrote, "I was appalled to read the article beside it by Jack Smith in which he refers to a firm of lawyers, a member of which is 'Ms. Meddlesome.' What a glaring example of the prejudice professional women must combat."

I hope it will not be thought that I am using Mrs. Green's letter in an attempt to discredit or even debate her point. I do regret that the mischievous name of Meddlesome should have turned up in exactly that context, giving Mrs. Green and perhaps other readers the impression that I am guilty of a prejudice which in fact I deplore in others and would despise in myself.

On the contrary, I have spent much of my own professional life under the supervision, more or less, of women editors, one of them being the remarkable Agness Underwood, who for several exuberant years was the very competent, very competitive, and very female city editor of the late *Los Angeles Herald-Express*. And now, once again, I find myself under the supervision of a woman editor, whose professional virtues I refrain from enumerating only because one of them is an imperviousness to sycophantic praise.

What troubles me is not Mrs. Green's very understandable inference about me, and her resentment of my supposed bias, but her use of the word appalled to describe the emotion I inspired in her.

In recent years, I have noticed, the word *appalled* has become indispensable among people who write letters to the editor to express disapproval of the newspaper, or one of its employees, or the government, or dogs and cats, or the Russians.

I would guess that one-third of all people who write the newspaper to say they don't like something describe themselves as appalled. The trend has snowballed in recent years, which makes me suspect that people who write letters to the editor also read letters to the editor and are influenced by each other's styles.

But I wouldn't be surprised if a study showed that *appalled* first began to turn up back in the 1960s. God knows the news was appalling. One might certainly be appalled by the assassinations, the body counts, the riots, the massacres and the many related calamities of that violent decade. (Not that the next one was much nicer.)

Literally, the word appall means to make a person grow pale. Thus, according to Webster's, a person who is appalled is "overcome with consternation, or dismay." And the word appalling, it says, means "inspiring horror, dismay or disgust."

I was appalled at the news of Kennedy's assassination; at the photographs of My Lai; at Kent State. I was appalled at Buchenwald, and am still appalled when I read of it today.

But, alas, I no longer know what word to give to such emotions, since appalled has been so trivialized. People are appalled now by the most bearable of life's imperfections, as their letters show: "I am appalled at the number of owls in the Hollywood Hills this summer." "I am appalled at your book reviewer's apparent lack of familiarity with the apocrypha of the *Bhagavad-gita*." "I am appalled . . ."

Of course two people may see the same thing in different ways, and I suppose one person could be appalled where another was merely apathetic. When I was a schoolboy my mother and my aunt went out to the movie one night and left my cousin Fred and me at home alone. My cousin was older than I was and rather a bad one. I had a secret and precocious talent at that time for drawing the comic strip heroine Tillie the Toiler in the nude, strictly from imagination; and to relieve the boredom of our homework my cousin prevailed upon me to turn out several examples of this art. Our mothers came home unexpectedly, as was their wont, and pounced upon some drawings of Tillie before they could be hidden. My aunt was appalled. My mother, on the other hand, was delighted that at last I had revealed some kind of talent.

So perhaps Mrs. Green was appalled. I'd like to think, though, that she was merely incensed, angered, offended, or disappointed.

Anyway, it's rather ironic. Meddlesome wasn't even that woman's name. It was just one of those unfortunate and inexplicable typos, and I take this opportunity of apologizing to Ms. Nettlesome for the error.

"John Cornell here," writes a former colleague, now retired, who lives in San Marino and keeps his hand in at the typewriter. "And I can't hold off any longer."

Cornell writes occasionally to sound the alarm against some new threat to the vigor and integrity of the language. Usually be is obliged, as we all are, to accept those changes and intrusions that he considers destructive. Not every enemy can be annihilated. The language is not a lake at Disneyland with controlled intakes and a pure bottom. It is a sea—turbulent, boundless, ever-changing. Nevertheless, some things get into it that are truly hideous, and they ought to be gaffed and done away with, before they make for the depths and start proliferating.

It is exactly such a monster as this that has brought Cornell to his post again, sounding general quarters. He has sighted that dreadful coinage—*workoholic*—and, worse, its even more dreadful cousins.

"When workoholic popped up recently in *The Times*," he confesses, "I almost pleaded with you for help. Now that *The Times* has sunk to the gawd-awful *gamble-oholic!*—I can't contain myself.

"If an addiction to alcohol makes one an alcoholic," he goes on in a rather pitiful appeal to logic, "an addiction to work would presumably make you a workic, if using the exact appendage is your passion.

"Use of virtually the whole word alcohol smacks of burning down the hut to roast the pig. The absurdity reaches new heights or depths in gamble-oholic, in which there's no attempt even to marry the two words. Just a hyphen. Are they trying to tell me *oholic* is a word or concept in its own right? Probably meaning something like gung ho? I don't find it in the dictionary. Is a happy sober man a wateroholic?"

I say Cornell's appeal to logic is pitiful only because it is doomed to fail, not because it isn't sound. For alas, Cornell's alarm has come too late, and in fact would not have saved us even if he had mounted the bulwarks and blown his bugle as the very first workoholic showed his barbarian head above the horizon. We are infiltrated already, and the thing can no more be repulsed by logic than a brush fire can be put out by stamping one's feet.

One hardly reads an edition of the paper or listens to a TV talk show without hearing that some public figure is a workoholic, or that the person talking is—in which case the word is delivered with a shy but defiant pride. Perhaps it has become popular in this mock confessional manner because the suffix *oholic*, with its echo of something quite deplorable, gives a tone of self-deprecation, however false, to what might otherwise come off as a boast. Ordinarily, modest people don't go about describing themselves as hard workers.

But perhaps I'm only trying to be logical, too. Who knows where workoholic came from, and why it multiplies? Someone said it first; someone overheard it and repeated it. It got onto radio, and into somebody's column, and on TV, and then—as the sportscasters say when the bomb is thrown and caught—goodbye!

The word's family has already begun to prosper with the mindless fertility of the infamous Jukes, producing ill-favored cousins such as *foodoholic* and such illegitimate marriages as *gamble-oholic*, which, as Cornell observes, brings together such unwilling partners that they have to be handcuffed by a hyphen.

Where does it stop? Will the devout be Godoholics? Will the lustful be sexoholics? Will we have dance-oholics, footballoholics, filmoholics? Will children who like toys be toyoholics?

The irony is that it was so unnecessary. For a long time in America it was enough to say of a man that he was a worker, or a gambler. Often, on Sunday afternoons when the family was being picked apart with the roast chicken, I heard my grandmother Hughes allow that some new and probationary in-law was a worker, which meant that he was also probably something else, such as a drinker or an Italian, but at least he could be counted on to provide. If she allowed that the fellow was a gambler, however, he might as well be struck by a thunderbolt: He was no good and his presence in the family would bring nothing but woe.

It was not even necessary to say *hard* worker, for emphasis. Everybody knew what a worker was; and as for compulsive gambler, my grandmother almost certainly didn't know the meaning of the word compulsive. A gambler was a gambler and a gambler was trouble. Who needed gamble-oholic?

All right. Cornell and I have answered the call to the colors. We will stand our ground. Never shall an oholic pass our barricade—unless he's an alc.

But we might as well preach against sin. The word has already metastasized and spread beyond eradication. The disease is inoperable. Nothing can save us now but a spontaneous remission.

Mark my words: Someday soon Cornell and I will be certified as wordoholics and burned at the stake by mobs of demented oholic-oholics.

THE EQUIVOKE

"Very interesting."

I had to be in San Luis Obispo to give a talk one evening last week and my wife drove up with me to enjoy the countryside. It is one of California's most agreeable drives, if you like seascapes, snowy mountains, green hills, old barns, live oaks, white rail fences, black cows and clean towns.

I gave my talk at Cuesta College, on the site of an old World War II Army post. Wooden barracks and other buildings that had once been occupied by soldiers were now in use by the college, and the auditorium in which I faced a friendly audience of perhaps four-hundred citizens of the community had once known the pandemonium of GIs applauding USO girls from Hollywood.

"Well, how did it go?" I asked my wife later.

"Fine, she said. "The audience was wonderful."

I wondered if that was an equivoke. Ever since learning what an equivoke was I had been listening for one. Though I had been using them all my life, I hadn't known they had a name until I found it in an essay by Norman Corwin in his luminous collection, *Holes in a Stained Glass Window* (Lyle Stuart, 1978). An equivoke is a remark that can be taken two ways: One seems to compliment the person it is directed at; the other satisfies the conscience and integrity of the person making the remark.

The most common and useful equivoke is the one made by persons who are obliged to comment on some object or work of art they find either incomprehensible or repulsive: "Very interesting."

Now, it seemed to me, my wife had used one on me. "The audience was wonderful." What did that really mean?

I was still puzzling over it the next morning as we drove down the Coast Highway toward home.

"You said the audience was wonderful last night," I said. "What about me? How was I?"

"You were the same as always," she said. "Why?"

It was not, I realized, a true equivoke; it was an evasion.

Its purpose, perhaps, was the same as an equivoke's—to please the one spoken to without telling an outright untruth or compromising the integrity of the speaker.

Her remark, while seeming to be directed to the question, was in fact evading it. An evasion simply won't do. An evasion is much easier to think up than an equivoke, for one thing, and is also more transparent. In the long run, it will be seen through, and one's good intentions will have gone for naught.

While Corwin did not coin the word equivoke, nor

invent the form, I give him credit out of humble gratitude. Except for Corwin's effort I might have gone on through life using and being used by equivokes without knowing what they were, just as most people use apophases without knowing what they are, and hyperboles, too, for that matter.

Equivoke obviously comes from the verb equivocate: "to avoid committing oneself in what one says," or the adjective equivocal: "subject to two or more interpretations...."

But as dictionary definitions often do, those fail to give the full intent, variety, and flavor of the well-turned equivoke, perhaps because it is better demonstrated than defined.

As Corwin shows us, the equivoke is epidemic in show business, and it's hard to see how actors, directors, producers and their hangers-on could stay on speaking terms at all without it. Equivokes are never more abundant than when the preview ends and the lights go up and all these people suddenly find themselves confronting one another.

One of Corwin's readers, screenwriter William Ludwig, submitted a number of the type used on these occasions, appending the second or true meaning in parentheses. For example:

"You couldn't have made this picture ten years ago. (Audiences would have wrecked the theater. Now they take anything.)"

Corwin himself gives us a few for that difficult bind we have all been in, when an artist we know shows us his latest work or a friend his latest acquisition, which turns out to be "an enormous wall-sized canvas painted entirely black except for a single green pea in the upper left corner."

The one we all fall back on, of course, is "Very interesting." But this is terribly threadbare, and not likely to fool a sophisticate of the kind who would paint or purchase such a work. Corwin suggests, instead:

"It makes me think of Miro. (Jerry Miro, a house painter from Carpinteria.)" Or else, "No one is going to take this lightly. (It must weigh a ton.)" Or, "This could start a movement. (Toward the door.)"

I rather like the Miro one, but it's a bit too clever, and would be sure to excite the artist's vanity and cause him to press for an elaboration which you are of course unable to provide.

Next to "very interesting" in popularity, I would guess, is "It certainly is different," which has the virtue of containing a truth even when "very interesting" may not. Of the same type, but given greater verisimilitude by a touch of current idiom, is this one: "That's really something else."

The feminist movement has mercifully eliminated one entire class of equivokes. No longer will a young man have to answer the question, "Do you think I'm pretty?" No liberated woman would ask such a question in the first place, and if she did a man would not be expected to equivocate. He would simply be expected to say yes.

One is in rather a worse predicament when asked by his hostess if he finds the Chicken Kiev good. If he wishes to be invited back he may not say simply "Yes," or even, "Yes, it's good," or even "Yes, it's very good." I myself wouldn't stop at anything short of "Yes, it's very, very good indeed!" But this is not an equivoke, even if true, and is very probably an outright lie.

It is a situation that calls for a true equivoke, something along the lines of, "Good! I'm afraid I've already eaten too much!" This not only gets you off the hook but makes it all right to ask for another glass of wine, for which, if it turns out to be a bit too acid, there are a number of standard equivokes.

I have borrowed lavishly from Corwin; but to borrow from Corwin is to praise him. And that's no equivoke.

A MANY-SLANDERED THING

Why do we call a flop a turkey?

Vivian Ringer, a friend of mine who has written exquisitely about women, and has such an affinity for Virginia Woolf that she once contrived to rent and live in that enigmatic lady's house for a spell, has complained to me about language that slanders and stereotypes not women, surprisingly, but animals.

She is troubled, for example, by such commonplace phrases as "it's a dog," meaning it's no good, a flop, a disaster. Though she didn't mention it, the phrase also appears as "she's a dog," a swinish male epithet for women they regard as hopelessly unappetizing.

Besides being a feminist, my friend also loves dogs. Her point, obviously, is that dogs are noble creatures, the embodiment of most of the virtues human beings cherish, and that to use the word as a metaphor for failure is a gross and illogical libel.

She is also irked by the use of turkey, as in, "it's a turkey," which is most often heard in disparagement of a play or movie and is universally understood to mean a failure, bust or flop. The turkey, she points out, is a lovely bird, and one which, I might add, is a symbol of Thanksgiving in our land.

How turkey got into the language as a metaphor for a theatrical disaster is evidently not known, since even William Morris, in his *Morris Dictionary of Word and Phrase Origins*, gives us only a dubious explanation from the Broadway composer Albert Hague, who said, "Turkeys are shows that open on Thursday night." How casually is a great bird slandered.

A more credible explanation is attributed to Groucho Marx, by Walt Keville of San Diego. "According to Groucho," he says, "it used to be widely believed that people simply would not go to plays and movies on Thanksgiving night. Theaters would react by showing second-rate productions, with second-rate casts. Since such productions were served to the public on Thanksgiving, they became known as turkeys. By extension, any bad play or movie became known as a turkey."

A different story, but still blaming the word on Thanksgiving, comes from Walter Collins of Newport Beach, who says he heard it one night at the Lambs Club in New York City when Bert Lahr, Bert Wheeler and Frank Fay were reminiscing.

"They told us that a producer had opened a Broadway show on a Thanksgiving night, not realizing that a big meal served in the middle of the day would bog most folks down to the point of not wanting to go out anywhere for anything for the rest of the day. They would hardly wish to get dolled up and go to the theater that evening, either. The producer (I think it was R. H. Burnside), when asked for an explanation as to why he had such a small house on his opening night, explained, 'Everybody was too full of turkey,' or words very close to that."

Richard Whiteman suggests that turkey as disaster makes sense if you look at it from the viewpoint of the bird itself. Just as surely as Thanksgiving will come, he is doomed. So a turkey is a show whose days are numbered. The ax will fall.

Yet another explanation comes from Norma Nichols of Van Nuys: "My husband, who is a musician and has played in back of a number of turkeys, should know. He says: 'A turkey cannot fly—therefore a turkey in the theater world is a show that never gets off the ground.' How can you refute such logic?" Simply as logic I can't, except on the ground that the premise is wrong. Turkeys *can* fly.

T. Jeanette Kroger of Walt Disney Productions quotes from "The Misunderstood Turkey," a piece she wrote for *Disney Magazine:* "The turkey is both an accomplished swimmer and flier. A turkey's air speed is about fifty-five miles per hour, and even on the ground, he has been known to keep well ahead of a galloping horse."

As for the bird's intelligence and character, she notes that Benjamin Franklin called the turkey "a bird of courage, a much more respectable bird than the bald eagle, and withal a true original native of America." Franklin opposed adoption of the bald eagle as our national symbol, by the way, because of its "bad moral character."

However it came by its name, the theatrical turkey may be given credit for producing a continual harvest of equivokes—those aforementioned two-sided compliments that flatter without compromising their author's honesty.

Judson O'Donnell recalls a summer theater play

he attended with Tallulah Bankhead and her then husband John Emery. "It was a complete disaster," he says. "An outrageous script, badly cast, and ineptly directed." But the cast was headed by a famous actress who was also a "bosom friend" of Tallulah's.

"Tallu writhed in her seat, appalled at the incredible performance unfolding before us. During intermission we agreed the play was utter torture, and Tallu was all for driving back to Manhattan at once and blotting out her memory at the Monkey Bar in the Hotel Elysée."

But Emery pointed out that the star knew that Tallulah was in the audience, and would expect her backstage after the show. "Tallu was stunned. What could she say to her friend? She could of course tell her the truth—that she had somehow managed to get herself into the worst turkey ever seen on the East Coast since the landing of the Pilgrims. Or she could lie and say the play and the star's performance were superb. But Tallu refused to tell the cruel truth. On the other hand, she refused to lie. What to do?"

The curtain mercifully descended. The three went backstage. The men hung back. The star was sitting at her mirror. "Tallulah didn't hesitate. She rushed over, joyously, throwing her arms around her friend. 'Dahling!' she roared in her basso profundo voice, 'Honest to Gawd, I've never seen anything like it!' Her friend beamed."

It is a mark of Tallulah's class that she didn't say, on this occasion, what Heywood Brown once said of her: "Don't look now, Tallulah, but your show is slipping."

Though she burned her candle at both ends, Tallulah lived to be sixty-five. But I doubt that anyone ever called her a senior citizen, or old, or anything but Tallu or Tallulah.

So much for the turkey. My friend Vivian is also disaffected by the misuse of language to abuse certain inanimate gifts of nature, such as the lemon. How industriously she tends her garden, how patient she is, how grateful when her little tree bears fruit, only to hold in her hand at last a symbol of ludicrous imperfection.

A lemon, in the idiom, is something that doesn't work. Yet what else is more suited to its niche in life, what other fruit is quite as indispensable? "Know'st thou the land where the lemontrees bloom.?" Is there any hint in Goethe's line that this tart delight, this prize for which the Crusaders invaded the Holy Land, would one day mean the same thing as Edsel?

I am not as sympathetic, though, toward my friend's disapproval of "weak as a kitten." It is true, as she points out, that it is almost impossible to detach a kitten from a sweater, once its claws are dug in. However, when I look at a kitten I am moved to remember Ogden Nash's melancholy reflection that a kitten eventually grows up to be a cat.

Whatever its strength, one is always bemused by how weak and helpless a kitten seems in comparison with the awesome cat it will all too soon become. I never pick up a kitten without an apprehensive vision of a crouching tiger, and I am constrained to be nice to the tiny thing, for fear it will spring to full size in an instant and disembowel me.

Even birds are maligned, my friend believes, in such phrases as "sing like a bird." To newer generations, that might appear to be a perfectly harmless simile. But those of us who lived through a gangster movie cycle of the 1930s know that to sing like a bird is to inform, to squeal, to betray one's pals. Such villainy is not to be found, as far as I know, among birds.

Of course many animal metaphors or similes are apt. Everyone knows someone who is dumb as an ox, or mean as a weasel. I don't know whether an ox is any dumber than a duck or a horse, but oxen certainly aren't very bright. (If they were, why would they form their plural by adding *en*, insteading of adding *es*, like lynxes, oryxes and foxes?)

Anyone who has ever worked with mules can understand "stubborn as a mule," yet this much-abused beast is far more intelligent than the horse. In fact, the reason it is so stubborn is that it is so intelligent. You would have to be dumb as an ox to do what the mule is asked to do without rebelling.

Much less appropriate than "stubborn as a mule" is "stupid as an ass," or simply "stupid ass." The ass, being father to the mule, is more intelligent than both the mule and the horse, and it is the ass that gives the mule its intelligence. So if you are going to call someone stupid, it is really unfair to asses to call him an ass.

My own favorite is "crazy as a loon," but I know it isn't logical. The loon may be noted for his plaintive cry, but otherwise, as far as I know, he is a bird that has his head on straight, although unhappy. I imagine the loon is thought to be crazy because "loon" is mistakenly associated with lunatic and loony, both of which come from luna, the moon; but loon is a Scandinavian word, and related to lament.

All the same, some of my best friends are as crazy as a loon, and some days, they say, so am I.

Katie Carlson of Marina de Rey is also irritated by the use of certain species of animals, or groups of people, as insults.

"I wondered aloud to myself," she writes, "at the seemingly innocent slur perpetrated upon ducks in a recent 'Peanuts' comic strip."

She enclosed the strip. It was the one in which Snoopy, the dog, admits he doesn't know what kind of bird Woodstock is, and says, "For all I know, you're a duck." This causes Woodstock to shed a tear, and Snoopy apologizes: "I'm sorry, little friend. I was hasty. You're not a duck."

What troubles Miss Carlson is this: "Why must we always refer to another group in order to create the maximum insult? Examples:

" 'You're as dumb as a Polack.'

" 'You act like an old woman.'

" 'You think like a Phi Beta Kappa.'

" 'If I didn't know you better, I'd think you were from New York.' "

Miss Carlson says she has a good idea why this is so, since she majored in college in the psychology of oppressed people, although at the time her father thought he was paying for a business education.

"The most successful way one group of people can be better or superior to another group, or all other groups," she says, "is to make sure that there is indeed an inferior one by saying it is so. This occurs on all levels: Democrats vs. Republicans; New Yorkers vs. Los Angelites; men vs. women; Catholics vs. Protestants; most seriously, whites vs. people of color; and now, birds vs. ducks."

As a result of Miss Carlson's betrayal of her father's hopes, we have lost a business executive, perhaps, but gained a social psychologist. And a good thing it is for ducks, too, since no one else appears to have come to that humble fowl's defense in this affair.

Of course the duck in "Peanuts" is merely a symbol of all the despised, oppressed, or merely laughed-at races, species and stereotypes. We know a bird doesn't have the intelligence to feel superior to a duck. But Charles Schulz, the cartoonist, has anthropomorphized Woodstock, giving him human perceptions and emotions. Snoopy on the other hand, being a dog, perhaps does know the difference between a bird and a duck, and has the sensitivity to know that he has hurt Woodstock's feelings. So he apologizes, but in doing so he implies that a duck is a lesser creature than a bird. So he has expunged his insult of Woodstock, but not his implied insult of ducks.

What concerns Miss Carlson is a cruel kind of humor in which a certain race, nationality or species is used as metaphor for some undesirable trait such as ignorance, cowardice or ineptitude. The Pole, whom Miss Carlson includes among her victims, has served as the embodiment of all three in a contemporary strain of ethnic humor which blessedly appears to be fading out.

Why this dishonor should have fallen on the Polish people is a mystery to me, since the Poles are richly endowed with precisely the opposites of those traits. Anyone who reads Romain Gary's novel of the Polish underground in World War II, *A European Education*, would find it hard ever to laugh again at a Polish joke and impossible to tell one.

But the very word Pole or Polish sets the listener up. It is going to be that kind of joke: "How many Poles does it take to screw in a lightbulb? Three. One to hold the bulb and two others to turn him around." As Miss Carlson says, the essence of this kind of joke (which I tell under poetic license) is that sweet sensation of superiority it gives to those other than its victims.

Ethnic jokes that inaccurately stereotype a group are not only despicable in themselves, but also they drive out good ethnic jokes. In the sensitive atmosphere of the past twenty years every kind of ethnic joke has become taboo, with the result that a great deal of legitimate humor has vanished from American social intercourse.

Leo Rosten's wonderful book, *The Joys of Yiddish*, shows on every page how vigorous and expressive that language is, and how illuminating, warm, and human the ethnic joke can be when it comes from insight instead of prejudice.

In speculating on the fate of my friend Gomez's parrot I have already told the story with which Rosten illustrates the phrase *aroysgevorian gelt*, meaning wasted money; an investment that does not prove fruitful; a gesture that goes awry. (It's the one about the two sons who give their frugal mother a talking parrot for company, only to have her tell them later that it was "delicious.")

That is an ethnic joke. It is about familial love, and frugality, and disaster, all of which are deep in the Jewish experience. As Rosten says, "A very large part of Jewish humor is cerebral. It is, like Sholom Aleichem's, reason made mischievous, or like Groucho Marx's, reason gone mad. . . . In nothing is Jewish psychology so vividly revealed as in Jewish jokes."

I will be glad when Polish jokes go out and true ethnic humor comes back in.

Meanwhile, let's not be beastly to the duck. Maybe he can't sing, but he is delicious.

FIRST THE WORD

"Supposing you thought yellow was brown."

It is a point of professional pride with me that rarely, in a long and perilous working life, have I been accused of misquoting anyone, including myself. So I was chagrined the other day by the following letter from a reader, Phil Davis.

"A man who thinks in quotation marks can't be all bad. In your column...you wrote: 'Oh, oh,' I thought, 'it's the poet and her mother.' Query: Did you really think 'oh, oh'? I've heard people say, 'Oh, oh.' Even whimper, whisper, groan, blurt, utter, mutter, sputter 'Oh, oh.' But to think 'Oh, oh'—that takes guts. Jack, believe me, an 'Oh, oh' thinking man is hard to find...."

Davis was referring to my report of an incident that had taken place one recent morning at my front door. That very day I had made a benighted criticism of a poem by a ten-year-old girl who lives down the street from us, and had answered the doorbell to find myself confronted by the girl and a determined-looking young woman. "Oh, oh," I thought, "it's the poet and her mother."

Davis doubts, evidently, that I thought any such thing. To argue the question would of course be idle, since Davis has no way of proving that I had no such thought, and I have no way of proving that I did.

I suppose all of us are tempted to improve on the thoughts we had in a given crisis, reshaping and ennobling them with hindsight. I sometimes question the honesty of generals, for example, who set down in their memoirs the humanitarian thoughts that occupied their minds on the eve of dreadful battles. Autobiography is the art of revision.

But Davis seems to doubt that people actually think in words and sentences, perhaps believing that language is not the essence of thoughts but only of speech.

No one knows exactly how we think, and no one knows exactly how language began. But there seems to be no doubt that the kind of complex and abstract thinking that distinguishes men from other creatures is not possible without language.

"It has even been argued," says the Welsh philosopher Richard Aaron, "that there can be no thinking without the use of language. It would seem difficult to deny, however, that men who are capable of thinking verbally need not always do so; intelligent thinking in a football player on the field is not necessarily verbal thinking. Nonetheless, it remains true that all human thinking is, for the most part, verbal."

That idea of course raises other questions. How much does language influence thinking? Was anyone in love before we had the word love? I imagine so.

Surely men and women were drawn to each other by the needs, feelings and impulses we call love long before the word itself was invented. But all the complexities that make love so blissful, so exasperating, so tenuous, would have been impossible. Love was not love until the first woman said, "You never say 'I love you' anymore."

I suppose Professor Aaron is right in guessing that intelligent football players sometimes act without thinking out their acts in words. Perhaps when Tony Dorsett runs between two converging tacklers, faking them out with a subtle change of speed and direction so they collide with one another instead of with him, he does not work in out in words first, but moves with the quick instinctive reflexes of a fish darting from the shadow of a predator. But most of the moves in football are the result of assignments, decisions and improvisations, and are probably activated by thoughts in words, such as "Oh, oh—that sumbitch hasn't got the ball! Now where the blip is it?" Without language man is a beast.

I not only verbalize my thoughts, I usually form the words silently with my speech equipment, so that I not only thought "Oh, oh!" that morning when the poet and her mother appeared at my door, but very probably formed the words without speaking them. Then, as I remember, I thought, "Say hello, you idiot," and immediately said hello.

Every conversation, excepting quarrels that get out of hand, is a game in which thoughts are first verbalized in the mind, then delivered in sound. Many first thoughts are discarded, once we see what they are, and others are quickly substituted. Thus at breakfast a husband may think "Jeez, is that what you call soft-boiled eggs?" But once the thought is fully formed and ready to go, it may, on second thought, be censored and something is thought up to take its place, such as: "How long did you cook these hard-boiled eggs?"

Marriage must have arrived much later in human history than love, for as the above scene suggests, it could not have existed without language. And, as my wife occasionally demonstrates, language is what makes it so precarious.

Oh, oh.

Though I was not previously aware of his work, a research psychologist named Julian Jaynes, at Princeton University, has duplicated some of my own thinking on the origin of consciousness in the breakdown of the bicameral mind.

In fact, *The Origin of Consciousness in the Breakdown of the Bicameral Mind* is the title of a book Jaynes published (Houghton Mifflin) in 1977. It wasn't an immediate best-seller, as one can imagine, but it is said to have had an "underground success."

I have not read the book, which is mercifully nicknamed *Origins*, but its tenets were described in an article by Richard Rhodes in *Quest* magazine, and a clipping has been sent to me by a reader who evidently noticed the parallels in my thinking and Jaynes's.

I'm sure I oversimplify, and perhaps I've got Jaynes wrong, but in essence I believe he is saying that man has become a conscious, introspective animal only recently in history, a very few thousand years ago, and that he crossed over into consciousness on words.

In another way of putting it, he invented consciousness by inventing metaphor and language. Before that, he simply ambled about like an automaton, or ape, moved to do this or that not by reflection and will, but by inner voices that he took to be the voices of the gods.

As I say, Jaynes's theory is much more complicated than that, or he wouldn't have had to write a whole book about it; but insofar as I understand what he's saying, I think he's right, even though many psychologists, according to the article, think he's wrong.

Like Jaynes, I have been thinking about thinking since I was a child, and I have never been able to get past the notion that it is impossible to think without using words. True, we do many things without describing our actions to ourselves in words; we do many things unconsciously. It has been my experience, for example, that you not only can't think how to tie your shoelaces—if you start to think about it you can't tie them at all. Try, sometime, to explain in words how you go about tying your shoelaces.

Knowing it is hard to think of man without consciousness, Jaynes points out that even today we are unconscious of many facts and functions of our daily lives. We are not conscious, for example, of the number of teeth in our mouths, of whether the door in a familiar room hinges left or right, of ourselves when watching television, or our actions when driving a car.

But I am fascinated even more by another facet of Jaynes's theory. Jaynes and I, by the way, are close to the same age, and this idea came to him when he was six years old, which is about when it came to me. Once again I am reminded of the almost simultaneous insights into the evolution of man by Charles Darwin and Alfred Russell Wallace.

"Were you an introspective child?" Rhodes asked Jaynes in the *Quest* article.

"Yes," Jaynes said. "I was a very introspective child. I had a whole other world that I never shared with anybody else. Not a fantasy world, but thinking about the mind, questioning. When I was six—I was supposed to be raking leaves—I stopped in front of a forsythia bush. The color yellow. It came to me with tremendous sadness that *I could never know, even though we had the same word, if another person saw the yellowness of those flowers inside his mind in exactly the same way I did. . . .*"

The italics are mine, to emphasize that I had almost exactly the same thought. (I may have been seven or eight.) Like Jaynes, I have been wondering about it ever since. Supposing you thought yellow was brown; that is, when you saw what I know as yellow, you called it yellow, but saw it as brown. You might also see what we both call red as more of a gray. The point is—neither of us would ever know that when we used the same word for a color we were talking about different colors.

I not only think it's possible, I think it is fairly well proved by the way some people dress. I have seen men wearing red neckties which I know they must have thought were blue. And for more than thirty years I have been studying a case right under my very eyes. I am now quite sure, though I cannot imagine any way of proving it, that my wife thinks purple is brown.

It isn't simply the purple rug in her bedroom. A woman is entitled to a purple rug in her bedroom. But she flaunts purple here and there—a scarf, a blouse, a skirt, a belt—with such abandon and disregard for matching accouterments that I can only conclude, her taste being fairly sound in other details, that she simply doesn't see purple the way most people do, or at least the way I do.

Except that I have given years of observation and introspection to this phenomenon, I might dismiss it merely as an eccentricity of taste, a bit of feminine mischief, rather than an actual aberration of color perception, a congenital flaw.

But if I hadn't long ago been sure about it, I would have been convinced the other day when she showed me the new pair of "sensible" shoes she's breaking in for our trip to England. Of course they're purple, but she has to think they're brown.

The only other answer I can think of is that what I call brown is actually purple.

ENGLISH-ENGLISH

"By the way, Heather, I've seen my solicitors."

A British linguist who fed a million words into a computer at Lancaster University has come up with the conclusion that Americans use the English language more correctly, according to the rules, than the British.

This will surely come as an incredible surprise to anyone who has ever watched an upper-crust British movie, read an English novel, or compared the speeches of Winston Churchill with those of Dwight D. Eisenhower.

In his project, Professor Geoffrey Leech studied newspapers, novels and government documents, among other kinds of writings, from both sides of the Atlantic. "The English language is the last great cultural legacy of the British Empire," he declared. "It is essential that we should be as fully informed as possible about the way English is being used in practice."

Professor Leech thinks, curiously, that Americans are more careful about the language because they are more "guilt-ridden" about it. On the other hand, the British more frequently use words associated with gentility and aristocracy, such as *sir, madam* and *gentlemen*, while an American is more likely to say *grandma*. "We (the British) are much more beset by doubts," he said. "The word *doubt* itself appears more frequently in our English and so does evidence that we tend to hedge our bets." (Anyone who has tried to penetrate a British triple negative will say hear-hear to that!) "*Ifs* and *buts, although* and *unless* are all more popular on this side of the Atlantic."

A parallel study has been made at Brown University, Providence, R.I., and I would like to wait until I see its findings before buying Professor Leech's conclusion whole hog (which an Englishman doubtless would never say).

Meanwhile, by a happy chance I have two letters by Englishmen on my desk, and in their different ways I think they elegantly exemplify the kind of clear, concise and graceful writing that is rarely found in the correspondence of American business or professional men.

One is from A. J. Maddock, curator of Thetford Museum, Norfolk, in answer to a letter from Raymond Pryke of Capistrano Beach, in which Pryke had offered to pay for cleaning Thetford's neglected statue of its embarrassing native son, Thomas Paine, the American Revolutionary firebrand.

Pryke explains to me that he saw the statue on the visit to Thetford, and was informed by the museum attendant that Paine was viewed as a traitor in England. "He further informed me that the entry of

Paine's birth in the parish record has been excised by some person or persons unknown. He also advised that the feeling in Thetford, even after two-hundred years, is very antagonistic toward Paine and his writing pamphlets and booklets in favor of the American Revolution."

When Pryke got back to Capistrano Beach from England he wrote the museum, making his offer, and received the following reply:

Dear Mr. Pryke:

Mr. Andrew, the museum attendant, has passed on to me the letter which you wrote to him concerning the statue. Your very generous offer to pay for the cleaning of the statue will be most appreciated, I am sure. However, I thought I should explain first what might be entailed, so that you can consider the terms of your offer, and then if you wish to go ahead I suggest you write to the Town Clerk, King's House, Thetford, Norfolk.

I understand that the local firm has offered to see to the cleaning of the stone plinth, but I gather that more than cleaning is required for the statue itself, which is of gilded bronze. It is said to need regilding with gold leaf, and estimates could run into thousands of pounds for this.

If you would like to write the Town Clerk, I am sure he will be able to give you all the facts you need.

Yours sincerely,
A. J. Maddock,
curator

Clear, brief, to the point, polite—and if you want to blow a few thousand pounds on the restoration of a traitor's statue, Yank, you're bloody welcome.

My wife and I, by the way, were briefly in Thetford on our recent tour of England, but we merely stood on the steps of the railroad station, waiting for a ride to the nearby village of Garboldisham. We had no idea that our hero Thomas Paine was held there in contumely, on a dirty plinth, and sadly in need of gilding.

The other letter was sent to me by Jake Zeitlin of Zeitlin & Ver Brugge Booksellers in Los Angeles, and though it comes from an esoteric world, I believe it is rather self-explanatory. At least I infer that Mr. Alan Thomas, its author, is also a bookseller, in London, and that the event referred to was an auction at Christies, and that *Lot 175 Appianus 1540* is a very rare ancient work that was on the block, and that Zeitlin and Thomas were expecting to be competing for its purchase.

The letter:

Dear Jake:
Re Christies today, *Lot 175 Appianus 1540*.

I marked my catalogue £10,000 to give. On the way to the sale I realized that the Queen would start for Parliament at 11 A.M. in the Royal Coach with a sovereign's escort of the Household Cavalry.

I thought: "There are thousands of books but only one Queen and I love her."

So I stayed to watch. When I got to Christies I learned that you had bought Appian for £8,000.
Greetings,
Alan Thomas

Few letters that essentially concern a business transaction can have packed so much drama, plot, suspense, patriotism, sacrifice and wistful disappoint-
ment into so few words.

I hope it is not too late for Professor Leech to feed
that one to his computer and say God Save the
Queen.

A reader in Santa Barbara named John del Valle,
evidently a man of philosophical temper, is bemused
by an odd juxtaposition of facts he found in a recent
issue of the *British Record*, a "review of British
affairs" published by the British Information Ser-
vices for the enlightenment of Americans.

The oddity that arrested del Valle's attention occurs in a column called "For the Record," on the
front page of the bulletin, and reads as follows: "The
United Kingdom, with the highest density of traffic
in Europe, has one of the lowest road accident
rates.... The pass rate for UK driving tests is still less
than 50 percent, more women than men fail it, and
British driving schools say schoolteachers are the
slowest to learn.... The wren has replaced the chaffinch as Britain's most common nesting bird."

Del Valle naturally wonders whether there is any
significance to the apparent linking of these two
statements (each undeniably significant in its own
right), or whether their juxtaposition is merely a
result of random chance.

He happens to be acquainted with two women
schoolteachers in Santa Barbara, one of whom is an
excellent driver, though he can't say as much for the
other. So there is nothing in his own experience to
verify conclusively the assertion that women and

schoolteachers make the worst drivers. He is even more puzzled by the news that wrens are being allowed to displace chaffinches as Britain's most common nesting bird.

That del Valle himself has tried rather hopelessly to relate these two facts in his mind is apparent from his letter, in which he seems to degenerate quickly from mere mystification into confused alarm.

"Surely," he writes, "the wrens aren't going to be allowed to take over every last common nesting site in England! Or to share them with lady schoolteachers who can't hack it as drivers. And if they should do this, where does that leave the chaffinches?"

I think I can put del Valle's mind at rest. What we have here, in the *British Record,* is a splendid little example of the English diplomatic genius for the timely diversion. This is a highly refined gambit, one that could have been developed only by the most civilized people, for introducing extremely provocative topics into polite conversation without allowing them to spoil tea.

I have been in Britain only once, but I have read a good many English novels, and I believe I am as familiar as most Americans with that most admirable of English social achievements, the drawing-room conversation. It is an art that we Americans, with our passion for frankness and combat—for taking the bull by the horns, as we say—have never been able to handle without breaking something, if only a teacup.

Thus, in the proper English novel, we find such passages as this:

"By the way, Heather, I've seen my solicitors. I'm suing you for divorce. More lemon, my dear?"

"I do believe, Edwin," she said, moving toward the great window and gazing out at the garden, "that the hollyhocks will be lovely this year."

Heather has got the news, all right, but she has adroitly changed the subject, thus averting what might have been a sticky scene, with the maid due any moment. There is nothing for Edwin to do, being a gentleman, but to go on about hollyhocks.

That is exactly what the *British Record* has done. Women and schoolteachers have just been told that they are the worst drivers in the United Kingdom, but no sooner do they catch their breaths at this affront than they are silenced by the news that the wren has replaced the chaffinch.

Now the ascendancy of the wren over the chaffinch is a subject that can be discussed by civilized men and women without passion or prejudice, and which, in the long view, is of greater consequence in the United Kingdom than the aptitude of women drivers. It is a matter, one can be sure, that will be debated politely, in the letters column of *The Times of London*.

What is happening, evidently, is that the wren has proven itself better adapted in the changing environment, and is displacing the chaffinch in a phenomenon known to ornithologists as "competitive exclusion." Two species that share the same ecology cannot share the same territory, and the weaker sooner or later will be run off by the stronger.

If I am not mistaken, it is the wren that has recently acquired the knack of prying the caps off milk bottles left outside the front doors of English dwellings, and this trick alone, perhaps, has given it a critical edge over its rival, the chaffinch, in their contest for domain.

My being English, I would be inclined to explore further the statement that women and schoolteachers make the worst drivers. I rather think that, if we were to toughen up our driving tests here in America, more women would fail than men; because, as even the feminists concede, women tend to be less respectful of tiny laws. Schoolteachers would also perform poorly, of course, because they tend to be absent-minded.

I wonder if anyone else has heard the hoot owl this autumn on Mt. Washington?

THE IRISH BULL

"I'd give my last dollar to be a millionaire."

He who wrestles with the English language is likely to find himself pinned when he least expects it, as I often demonstrate unconsciously. Now and then, trying to manhandle an idea that may be clear enough in our heads but hard to tie down with words, we come up with one of those engaging mutations known as bulls.

I would have thought the word bull in this sense was pure slang, and of recent origin; but the *Oxford English Dictionary* cites its use as far back as 1640, and notes that in 1711 the poet Alexander Pope, in a letter to a friend, admitted having committed one himself: "I confess it [is] what the English call a bull, in the expression, tho' the sense be manifest enough."

Robert A. Fowkes, professor of Germanic languages at New York University, has noted in the language quarterly *Verbatim* that the bull is often called Irish because Irish seem to have a special gift for it. Professor Fowkes cites one definition of an

Irish bull as "a saying that contradicts itself, in a manner palpably absurd to listeners, but unperceived by the person who makes it."

Perhaps the best distinction between an Irish bull and most other bulls was that made by a Professor Mahaffy of Dublin University when a lady asked to be enlightened on that point: "An Irish bull," the professor replied, "is always pregnant."

Professor Fowkes cites several examples from the great literature of the bull, such as this one: "He lay at death's door, and the doctor pulled him through." And a jury's verdict: "We find the man who stole the horse not guilty."

The bull often turns up in impassioned oratory, as here: "Such is the corruption of the age that little children, too young to walk or talk, are rushing through the streets cursing their Maker." It is likely to lurk in pompous parental lectures: "The trouble with you, my son, is you've no respect for the father that gave you birth."

A truly American bull was produced recently by the police department of a New Jersey town, striving for equality of opportunity, in this announcement: "From now on we shall offer police jobs to qualified women regardless of sex." And it was the state of New Jersey, the professor says, that once made the following bullish law: "If two cars approach at right angles at an intersection where there is no traffic light, each shall make a full stop and wait until the other has passed by."

I find that the bull is also dealt with by Professor William S. Walsh in his fascinating and invaluable *Handy-Book of Literary Curiosities*, first published in 1892. He notes that Sydney Smith, the great English wit, called the bull the very reverse of wit: "For as wit discovers real relations that are not apparent, bulls admit apparent relations that are not real."

Even Shakespeare committed bulls, Professor Walsh observes, as well as the impeccable Dr. Johnson. But the professor holds that the only great bulls are Irish: "To the right perpetration of the bull there seems to go a kind of innocent and almost rollicking wrongheadedness, which has no real counterpart outside the Irish race. The Irish animal is lively, rampant, exhilarating, like the sprightly hero of a Spanish bullfight, while English and other bulls are mere commonplace calves blundering along to the shambles."

He recalls the Irish gentleman, wanting singing lessons, who was told the first lesson would be two guineas, and all thereafter one guinea each. "Oh, bother the first lesson," he said. "Let us begin with the second."

Also there was the Irish officer who told a friend on arrival in Calcutta: "India, my boy, has the finest climate under the sun; but a lot of young fellows come out here and they drink and they eat, and they drink and they die; and then they write home to their parents a pack of lies, and say it's the climate that has killed them."

But Professor Walsh, like Professor Fowkes, takes his hat off finally to one of the bulls that seem to come so easily to American bureaucracy, citing a resolution by a Canton, Mississippi, city council. "Resolved, that we build a new jail. Resolved, that the new jail be built out of the materials of the old jail. Resolved, that the old jail be used until the new jail is finished."

Professor Fowkes isn't sure, but he thinks it may have been Groucho Marx who observed, "Even the future ain't what it was in the past."

"I have for many years been an admirer of the Irish bull," writes Bob Abernethy of NBC news. "Once an Irishman in London went up to the railroad ticket window breathlessly and said, 'I suppose the next train for Reading has left already?'"

Abernethy also recalls a day he and his wife were taking a bus tour of Dublin. "As we passed the Dail, the Parliament building, the guide explained, 'The back of that building is in the front, and you're looking at the other side of it now.'

"My favorite, I guess," Abernethy adds, "is attributed to an Irish politician in the heat of debate who shouted, 'I'm not a bird—I can't be in two places at once.'"

Karin Franks of Pasadena also offers a genuine Irish bull that was inspired by a rugby game at Trinity College in Dublin. "Suddenly the ball landed in the grandstand. There was a little delay. The boys called 'The ball! The ball!' A voice from the grandstand called back, 'To hell with the ball, get on with the game!'"

"I deny they're Irish," writes Alfred Connor Bowman of Hermosa Beach, "until someone proves it. I regard them as, rather, part of the Yiddish tradition of Eastern Europe, transplanted to the Bronx and Brooklyn. That's where I met them, through the bountiful agency of a Jewish head janitor who always had one to cheer me up when he caught me working late on Governor's Island. My favorites include:

" 'I'd give my last dollar to be a millionaire.'

" 'Better be well for ten years than sick for one day.'

" 'Better to have a hundred friends than one enemy.'

" 'An old man should never be born.' "

John Purtle writes, "I read an ad (for a television set) which contained these sentences: 'The color is unbelievable. You have to see it to believe it.' "

"This afternoon," writes Hal Hennacy of San Marino, "when sending a check to my son to aid him in his travels in France, my closing line in the accompanying note was: 'Attached is a check in the amount of $100. Please let me know if it doesn't arrive.' Is that an Irish bull?"

No, Mr. Hennacy, that is a San Marino bull.

"I would like to contribute a local example of that self-destruct," says Ed Deverill, a San Diego City Council administrative assistant. Some years ago one of our more earnest councilmen was struck by an innovative idea for cutting costs in the Fire Department. Dismayed by the high rate of false alarms, he recommended, in a deadly serious memorandum, that the city manager 'investigate the feasibility of using only obsolete fire equipment to answer false alarms.' "

Donovan Roberts, a newspaperman who used to cover the wondrous Los Angeles County Board of Supervisors, treasures his recollections of the late Frank G. Bonelli's way with English. "These samples," he says, "may give you and the indifferent public some idea of the Bonelli touch. That is to say, the Italian input.

"There was the occasion when Frank wanted to praise his fellow supervisor, Ernie Debs, for a job well done. This came out as his wish to praise Mr. Debs 'for the dogmatic way he pursued this subject.'

"It must be understood that Frank did not knowingly err—he merely tried to improve the available words."

Roberts's favorite goes back some years to when a Presidential commission on the drug traffic held a hearing in the supervisors' board room, and Bonelli, as chairman, gave them an oratorical welcome. "I am sure," he concluded, "that this commission will do an infinitesimal amount of good."

"You know something?" says Roberts. "He was exactly right."

I suppose Bonelli's boners should be called malapropisms, rather than true bulls. But why quibble? They are works of art, and ought to be remembered even if they're forgotten.

WE MISS YOU, HARRY TRUMAN

"Money isn't everything, but it's everything else."

Since Harry Truman left the scene, we have not heard much plain language from our political figures. It is the age of gobbledygook and nospeak, although Ronald Reagan is a good man with a quip. Otherwise the official pronouncements pulsing out over the nation on the airwaves are as homogenized as our milk.

It might be argued that the locker room language of Watergate was colorful, as revealed in the tapes, but to me it seems merely crude, murky and witless.

I suppose that here and there around the country a region is entertained and enlightened by some local politician with a gift of imaginative speech, but we are not likely to hear it from the White House again.

As we have already recalled, the late Los Angeles supervisor Frank Bonelli could bring a moment of enchantment to the ordinarily dull proceedings of that body, as when he praised a colleague for his dogmatic work.

Another regional hero who appears to have been of Bonelli's metal was Anthony Brandenthaler, a rough-hewn lumberman who came out of the sawmills to run Oregon's centennial celebration back in 1959. I'd never heard of Brandenthaler, but a man who collects such things, George O. Morrison of Monrovia, has sent me a clipping about him from the *Portland Oregonian* of October 11, 1959. It was written by *Oregonian* reporter Harold Hughes, who obviously felt his obligation to posterity.

Tony Brandenthaler's special field was the mixed metaphor, or Tonyism, as Hughes called it. They fell from his lips like timber crashing in the forest. As chairman of the centennial commission, Brandenthaler found himself in what he called "a maelstrom of baloney," and complained that there were "too many cooks in the fire."

"Tonyisms were always fired point-blank," Hughes recalled, "without aim, right off the Brandenthaler hip. Some of the more lethal remarks fell into the category of blue-flame aphorisms and are thus lost to all except private collectors."

Brandenthaler tried to fight his way out of his maelstrom of baloney with directness and simplification. To illustrate a complicated fiscal problem he told his bewildered colleagues, "Take nine horses at $50,000 apiece." A man with a complaint was turned away with, "You're making a mountain out of a mole."

With a flair reminiscent of Sam Goldwyn, he condemned an old building on the exposition grounds as a "sore eye," and admitted one of his own errors of judgment by saying: "I voted like a sore thumb."

His philosophy could be both cynical and practical

at once. "Money," he told a bemused commission, "is like the eleventh commandment. If you don't have the money, the other ten commandments are of no avail." Or to put it another way, as he did, "Money isn't everything, but it's everything else."

When the going was uncertain, Brandenthaler would say, "We've got to play this by tune." To fight adversity, he attacked with mangled aphorisms in his booming lumberman's voice. "Like Sherman said, 'This is a hell of a war!'"

Filling reporter Hughes in on a divided commission meeting, Brandenthaler said, "We were sitting there like loggerheads." But he assured the reporter it was "neither on the record nor off the record."

In desperate straits he shouted defiance. "This is Custer's Last Rally! I'll go down dying with my two hats and shoes on."

As rough and raucous as Brandenthaler might be, he was not unfair. "Let's not cut up Uncle Charley until we get a new suit on him," he would say. He was not inflexible. "I have changed the temple of my thinking."

Deep down, he believed in the centennial. He didn't want his fellow Oregonians to "sit on their heritage and rust."

Brandenthaler's friends and colleagues collected his Tonyisms, picking up and hiding them away like dropped pearls. "Each was a sparkling legacy to the state's centennial celebration," Hughes wrote, "and valued far more than all the souvenir plates and ashtrays imported from England and Japan."

For posterity, Brandenthaler himself put his gift in perspective, "Don't take everything I say so verbally."

What most American communities lack, it seems to me, is a central figure of Brandenthaler's stature—

a man in charge, a John Bunyan of a man who could rally us all like Custer, cut through the maelstrom of baloney, and go down dying, if necessary, with his hats and shoes on.

I know Hughes will understand when I say we are grateful to him for his dogmatic reporting of Anthony Brandenthaler's wit and wisdom. For those who cherish truth, its worth is infinitesimal.

As the language of American politics declines, we should be ever more thankful to those few dedicated journalists who have taken care to preserve some of the great moments from the age of rough-hewn individualism and the self-made man.

The recent vogue for the words of Harry Truman as entertainment is obviously a symptom of our nostalgia for a language whose point was always clear, however misbegotten its imagery and syntax.

Another man with a gift like Brandenthaler's in kind, if not in size, was James McSheehy of the San Francisco Board of Supervisors, whose inimitable coinages have been reverently collected for posterity by such San Francisco newspapermen as Michael Harris, Dick Chase and Charles McCabe. In a story written on the one-hundreth anniversary of McSheehy's birth, Harris recalled some of the spontaneous locutions with which the supervisor routinely galvanized constituents and colleagues alike.

"Ladies," he once said to a group of housewives, speaking as the chairman of the finance committee, "I have here some figures which I want you to take home in your heads, which I know are concrete."

Speaking out against an ill-conceived construction project, McSheehy warned his fellows: "This has all the earmarks of an eyesore."

Facing up to a melancholy problem that municipalities have had to deal with since the earliest times, McSheehy asked: "Where will we get the money to bury the indignant dead?"

Always the financial watchdog, McSheehy opposed a particular budget request with the opinion, "They don't need that much money for the next physical year." And of another dubious project he declared, "It would be like carrying coals to Mohammed."

Whatever his weaknesses, it could not be said that McSheehy was afraid to speak his mind. "Let's call a shovel a shovel," he would say, "no matter who we hit."

McSheehy had a gift not only for expressing practical ideas, but also for philosophical flight. He could soar, "Let us put our shoulder to the wheel," he once exhorted, "and help the Ship of State to sail down Market Street."

As "the most splendid McSheehyism of them all," columnist Charles McCabe nominated an apothegm which, as he pointed out, incorporated all the essentials of public life: "You can't straddle the fence and still keep your ear to the ground."

My own favorite is a remark McSheehy interjected into an hour-long debate on whether the city should buy six gondolas, to be imported from Italy at a cost of several thousand dollars, for a lake in Golden Gate Park. "Gentlemen," suggested the always penurious McSheehy, "why spend all that money? Why not just buy two of them and let nature take its course?"

More recently the New Jersey State Senate was blessed with the presence of a gifted member, Anthony Imperiale, whose extravagances have been preserved as a part of that state's heritage by political columnist Neil Lewis. Like McSheehy, Imperiale watched pennies in behalf of his constituents. "They're fed up," he told his colleagues, "with exuberant taxes." And in advocating passage of a tax reform bill, he promised: "It will go a long way toward nipping the bull by the horns."

Occasionally Imperiale brought off a truly stupefying comment. One of this magnitude came out in debate on a proposed code of ethics. The senator asked whether the code would speed construction of Newark Airport, a question whose relevance his colleagues did not immediately grasp. Was there not, the senator reminded them, a dispute over how many minority workers should be hired on the airport job? Then did it not follow that "this code of ethnics might solve the problem?"

Back in the 1960s, when the San Francisco supervisors were debating whether to spend $55,000 for a wind study of Candlestick Park, columnist McCabe proposed that the money be spent on a wind study, but not at Candlestick.

"I am frankly worried about the decline of political oratory," he said. "Our supervisors . . . are about as eloquent as Calvin Coolidge in a shower. . . . So let's have that wind study. But in the right place. Candlestick is hopeless. Maybe we can reclaim the supervisors. Some of the $55,000 could be diverted to an award of the annual James McSheehy Medallion for Oratory."

A fine idea. Perhaps we could have a national hall of fame for the likes of McSheehy, Brandenthaler, Imperiale and Bonelli; a place where their words could be graved in stone, and as McSheehy himself once said, "their roosters could come home to hatch."

LOVE IS ENERVATING

"Only the lion and the cock withstand love's shock."

In times like ours, when there are few restraints on language, even in what used to be called mixed company, the graceful euphemism, the double entendre, and even the risqué remark are disdained as old fashioned, and a person who enjoys such devices is thought quaint, as if he collected old bottles or antimacassars.

Perhaps that is why my occasional attempt to write of sex as if it were still a subject to be dealt with delicately gets me into trouble with readers who don't know what I'm driving at.

"I am puzzled," writes Judy Wilson, for example, "by your use of the word enervating. You wrote, 'nor were my libidinous petitions ever rewarded by anything more enervating than a frank look of interest in a pair of dark blue eyes, a provocative smile or a meaningful giggle.'

"In that context it is hard to imagine anything enervating being much of a reward. My aged

Webster's gives as a second definition: 'to lessen the moral vigor of,' and it has occurred to me that you may retreat behind that definition after seeing how many of your faithful readers were not too enervated to write. . . ."

I don't know why Miss Wilson should be puzzled by the word enervate in that passage, nor, indeed, why she should think I might need Webster's No. 2 definition to justify its use. The first definition, in the *New Collegiate*, is: "to lessen the vitality or strength of," and that will serve quite well, I think, to define the phenomenon I had in mind.

I was writing about going to summer school when I was a boy, and how I loved it because there were always more girls than boys. But even though the odds were so excitingly in my favor, and I knew one ought to strike while the iron was hot, the iron was not yet hot. Summer's end found me quite as innocent of sexual fulfillment as its beginning.

I suppose I erred, thus causing Miss Wilson's puzzlement, and perhaps that of other readers, in attempting to clothe rather an intimate revelation in demure attire, so that it might appear in the most decorous company without offending anyone.

To be candid, I was trying to say that summer school's delicious disproportion of the sexes, as advantageous as it seemed, did not in the long run catapult me into that ultimate experience which I knew to be, from my reading, quite enervating.

Without drawing from my own subsequent experience, I may point out that literature is replete with allusions to the enervating effects of requited love, and poets could no more think of passion without languor than of day without night. Since ancient times they have sung of the sweet lassitude that is the aftermath of love's frenzied consummation, and one of its rewards.

"The strongest," said Shakespeare, "love will instantly make weak."

Though the enervation of which I speak has been celebrated in a thousand more melodious lines, none go straighter to the point than these of Oliver St. John Gogarty:

> *Only the Lion and the Cock,*
> *As Galen says, withstand Love's shock.*
> *So, dearest, do not think me rude*
> *If I yield now to lassitude,*
> *But sympathize with me. I know*
> *You would not have me roar, or crow.*

What astonishes me about that verse, in fact, is that a chap in its author's enervated condition would have had the vigor to compose it on the spot, when what he obviously wanted was to sleep.

As long as I have been drawn into these perilous waters, I might as well take up another query, from Ellie Pietsch of La Mirada, who writes to ask if I can interpret a quotation she found in an interview with Louise Fletcher, by Roderick Mann, as follows:

"Only the last love of a woman can satisfy the first love of a man."

"As our office staff consists of a psychologist, nurse, teacher, speech and language specialists," says Miss Pietsch, "and none of us could really determine what the heck this is supposed to mean, perhaps you can get the real meaning for us. I only hope it's not too risqué or trivial for your column."

I don't know what the quotation means. But I do know that it is neither too risqué nor too trivial for this space. What we have here, in fact, is an excellent example of one of the most ancient devices of rhetoric. If you want to say something that will be thought neither trivial nor risqué, make sure it is too vague to be understood at all.

I do know one thing, though. Whether it's your first love or your last, it's enervating.

COLLECTORS' ITEMS

*Her own mother was
ravished before dinner.*

If I were at all inclined to collect something, as some
people collect dolls or pipes, I think I would collect
malapropisms, also known, as we have seen, as Pullet Surprises.

Offhand I can think of few fruits of the creative
process that are more thoughtlessly wasted. It isn't
that they aren't plentiful. Almost all of us can make
one without trying. They seem to fall from our lips
like leaves from a tree, but alas, they are no sooner
airborne than they blow away to be lost forever. They
pass unnoticed, like Thomas Gray's flower, born to
blush unseen.

But at least one person in Los Angeles not only has
an ear for malapropisms, she saves them, not to be
used again, but to be kept and treasured like rare
stamps.

Eleanor Schohl's collection is authentic. Each speci-
men is one she actually heard at the moment of its

birth, not one she picked from a book, or someone else's collection. Only those delivered innocently in a real conversation are to be trusted. Malapropisms that are deliberately thought up, no matter how clever the writer, never have the true metal ring of those that are wrought in the heat and tension of spontaneous speech.

Perhaps that is why the malapropisms of the original Mrs. Malaprop, who gave her name to the form, have always seemed wooden and artificial to my ear, compared with the unaffected gems dropped by my own mother, for example. Mrs. Malaprop's malapropisms could be no better than those of the playwright who created her, and the best of them was her reference to the headstrong allegory that lives on the banks of the Nile.

What makes that one so amusing, I suppose, is the fact that the large amphibious reptile found along the banks of the Nile is not an allegory at all, but a crocodile. A part of the malapropism's charm is the slight sense of superiority it gives to the one who hears it uttered. Just the other night I was delighted to hear a TV sports announcer say that a player was trying to attune for his error.

The really great malapropisms not only sound very close to the word intended, but have a kind of logic of their own. One of Mrs. Schohl's, for example, is in this overheard remark: "It's too soon to have lunch. I want to starve him off for awhile." In this context, "starve" not only makes as much sense as "stave," but more.

Mrs. Schohl has also collected this one: "It was spreading like wildflower." Actually, that one is not unique. I have heard it myself. The word intended, of course, is "wildfire," meaning something that spreads rapidly and destructively. Here, again, though, the malapropism might be in some contexts an improvement, especially when whatever it is that's spreading is not destructive. Might it not be said that in the spring young love spreads like wildflower?

Mrs. Schohl has also heard someone say a family was going to "pick up sticks and move." I suppose "pick up stakes" was meant here, a term derived from the pioneer practice of staking out a homestead; but today perhaps "sticks" makes more sense. Many a family, hit by a run of bad luck in what it hoped would be a greener field, might well see its household as reduced to sticks.

"It gets to be a dredge on the market."

Mrs. Schohl doesn't recall what it was that had become a dredge on the market, but it might have been anything from porno flicks to limousines. The word intended here, evidently, was "drudge," meaning a bore.

I leave it to the reader to discover the sense below the superficial error in these others from the Schohl collections:

"We have to paint ourselves out of this corner."

"I'm not a hate mongrel."

"I don't think he conscientiously tried to deceive me."

"It gives you pause for thought."

"Some cops were paroling around."

"She went out like a kite."

"You try to install it in your children."

I have never understood how these appealing verbal accidents come to life in the human mind. I simply assumed that some people had a gift for them, like Mrs. Malaprop herself.

But now I have heard from George C. Tyler, a medical doctor, who offers a fascinating theory about their origin. "Malaprops occur," says Dr. Tyler, "because of transient drops in the oxygen level of the brain's speech center, since they tend to pop out often in long sentences, or from people who talk a lot instead of breathing deeply and listening a lot.

"Also," the doctor continues, "they seem to occur often at cocktail parties, where a lot of people are breathing deeply and talking. I also think that reading malaprops can occur. For example, I was holding my breath trying to drink coffee and read your article (without chortling and strangling) and twice read 'large ambiguous reptile.' "

Dr. Tyler is referring, of course, to my mention of Mrs. Malaprop's "the headstrong allegory that lives on the banks of the Nile."

I would like to put Dr. Tyler's mind at ease. It is no wonder he thought he had read "large ambiguous reptile," for the allegory is indeed a large ambiguous reptile, and the word "amphibious," I must confess, was a topographical error.

Dr. Tyler's theory seems to bear out my own theory that a first-rate malaprop cannot be contrived. Besides, when you make one up, for fun, you can never prove afterward that you did it deliberately. People prefer to think you're dumb. I now regret having used the phrase "a drudge on the market" just to prove that I could think up a malaprop if I wanted to. I have received no less than a dozen letters pointing

out that the proper phrase is "a drug on the market."
What a drudge.

Just in the last few days friends of mine have
reported hearing that prices in the supermarket were
absorbent, that a hospital patient was being put in
tension, and that an Episcopalian from Kansas City
was surprised to see incest on the altar at a church in
the Wilshire district.

Larry Black of Pacific Palisades recalls a friend
who was telling him about a poor boy who worked
his way to the top. "It's a regular Alger Hiss story,"
the friend said. A colleague of mine, Bart Everett,
recalls a Trans World Airlines dispatcher who announced, "To all intensive purposes" and a training
sergeant at Ft. Dix who told his recruits they were
about to experience a "stimulated attack."

Michael Mandell of Sherman Oaks writes that his
wife Louise has given him permission to reveal her
most famous work: "Make up your mind, Michael—
which side of the fence are you straddling?"

Once in a while a true genius turns up, and lucky
indeed, I would say , is the man who has one for a
wife. I am unable to conceal my envy of another
colleague, Barry Zwick, whose wife Bobbie is extra-
ordinarily gifted and prolific.

Mrs. Zwick, for example, once observed that a
person with a tumor must go in for an autopsy. She
also refers to small, low-slung German dogs as Dat-
suns. In Alaska, she says, they have token poles.

In the Middle Ages, says Mrs. Zwick, Europe was
hit by the platonic plague. Young people in yellow
robes who chant on Hollywood Boulevard are dis-
ciples of Harvey Kushner. *Rain* was written by

Somerset Mong and *Arrowhead* by Sinclair Lewis. Water is painful when it's scowling hot, and Solzhenitsyn was exported from the Soviet Union.

Zwick surely is among the happiest of men.

All the same, even malaprops can become a drudge on the market, and if Mrs. Zwick were my wife, I'd tell her to breathe deep and do more listening.

Meanwhile Bob Stivers writes from his bed in Hoag Memorial Hospital, Newport Beach, to protest my listing "tension" as a malapropism for "traction," quoting a person who said she had a friend in the hospital in tension. It happens that Stivers is in tension, and he doesn't think it's just a malaprop.

"I am recovering from nerve damage in my back which affects the strength and motion of my left leg," he writes. "The present treatment consists of remaining in traction for several weeks. I regularly call the nurses on the intercom and ask to be put into tension or removed from tension. The latter is undoubtedly a wish that remains unfulfilled. The nurses merely respond by placing or removing fifteen pounds from the pulley. They do not realize that many of their other actions are more effective for placing me in tension—such as not getting me a morning *Times,* or refusing my wife a cup of coffee, interrupting pro football games, and so on."

I report this case not only to bring this poor man into contact with the outside world, but also because it illustrates one of the most desirable qualities of the true malaprop. Like "tension," it ought to make more sense, in context, than the word for which it was innocently substituted.

I don't like to make too much of this, without further study, but the evidence seems to suggest that women have much more felicity with the mala-propism than men. They are of course the wittier of the sexes, and perhaps their malapropisms are simply unconscious shoots of the wit that a male society has traditionally required them to keep plowed under. Or maybe not so unconscious.

David Khan reports that his wife utters malaprops as naturally as she breathes, and in complete in-nocence. She fears that Russia will push us to the brim; she complains that someone has her up a barrel; that the sky is overhung; that one of her husband's friends is a regular San Juan; that every one has his hangovers (evidently meaning hangups).

Meredith Hale reports a landlady who was scorn-ful of wistful thinking; a sister-in-law who buttons down the hatches before a storm; and an elderly neighbor who fears she is going berkshire. Mrs. Hale's own mother once announced before dinner that she was ravished.

Ernestine Stellman's daughter is always resolving to turn into a new leaf, a little work of malapropic art that is now a family heirloom. Cynthia Aldendifer says her mother is good for two or three malaprop-isms a day. "Today, on long distance, I said, 'I hope you've been having a lot of rain,' and she said, 'Oh, my goodness, yes. It's so dark here you could cut it with a fork.'"

Boyd H. Wessman says his sister-in-law reported that a young woman exuberating over her gifts at a bridal shower was most delighted with the ostracizer.

Wendy Reid Crisp has a grandmother who is always getting her dandruff up, or doing something on the spare of the moment, and comes home worn to a fragile. Dorothy Anderson's sister has a neighbor who picked a lawyer out of the phone book at ransom. Flora Hoover has a friend to whose house the ants come in groves. Jo Bettitt's former mother-in-law had a black dress covered with sequences and was taking sympathetic hormones. Lillian Sturbergh had a neighbor whose husband sometimes didn't munch words.

Yes, men can do it too. But it helps if they have a Middle European accent, like Jason Wingren's late theatrical agent, Leon O. Lance. Lance always called him Greenspring, and at their first meeting told him Scream Gens had an absolutely fireproof part for him. But later, Lance said Greenspring didn't get the part because the producer didn't know him from Adams.

So enough already. Let's all turn into a new leaf before we're worn to a fragile.

POINTLESS PROVERBS

Everything makes sense.

English periodicals apparently are trying to divert their readers from the ghastly news of the season with amusing games and contests.

A page from a recent issue of the *New Statesman* reports on readers' entries in a competition for the most "profound-sounding but pointless proverbs."

I would think that any number of excellent profound-sounding but pointless proverbs could be gleaned from the pages of *Bartlett's Familiar Quotations* or any other anthology of wisdom, since pointless profundity is one of the most abundant products of the human mind.

Publilius Syrus, a Latin versifier of the first century B.C., encapsulated almost all popular wisdom in several hundred proverbs, e.g., "To do two things at once is to do neither." He was also the author of "A rolling stone gathers no moss," and "You should hammer your iron when it is glowing hot." However, you can't hammer your iron as often as Publilius did without striking off an inferior piece now and then, a truth of which my own efforts offer abundant evidence.

For example, Publilius advises, "Do not turn back when you are just at the goal." Good advice generally, to be sure, but in football a receiver who is at the goal may have to turn back to receive a pass that is short. This is a truth that I myself would express, for general application, as "Any gain is better than an incompletion."

Just as the touchdown is often lost because the pass is a step too short, it is very easy to miss profundity by a very short distance, and the failure is hard to explain. On the other hand, it is almost equally hard to invent a mock aphorism that doesn't have some truth in it. Truth is the most mischievous of entities. It eludes those who seek it and visits those who would avoid it.

As the person who conducted this competition for the *New Statesman* noted (a Ms. de Meanor, by the way), "Meaning was a real problem [among the entries]. It kept slipping in. Still, a fair few managed to sound convincingly gnomic while remaining outstandingly pointless."

A number of the entries are published by the *New Statesman,* and my favorite among them is "Beggars can't be existentialists." It certainly sounds profound, but I have no idea what it means, and it probably means nothing, which would make it a winner.

Still, it may mean nothing to me only because I have never understood what existentialism is. There is no use trying to tell me, either. I have read novels, plays and autobiographies by existentialists and seen existential movies, and I still don't know what existentialism is. Frankly, I'm happy to observe that the word seems to have gone out of vogue. Evidently, whatever it was, it didn't work.

Even so, it might mean something, and if it does, it might be something that beggars can't be. In that case, "Beggars can't be existentialists" is profound after all and must be disqualified in the competition. You see how difficult it is to say anything without meaning something?

But the difficulty becomes ever more evident as we examine some of the other entries reported by Ms. de Meanor. For example: "A wise man does not need a chain saw to serve a blancmange." At first glance, certainly, that appears to be meaningless. But regard the opposite: "A wise man needs a chain saw to serve a blancmange." That is so obviously not true that its opposite must be true. One might propose the following aphorism to express this particular phenomenon: "Whatever is not not true must be true."

Here's another from the competition: "One man's catch is another man's wicket." That obviously is related to the game of cricket, and consequently beyond the understanding of the American mind— even my own, which is well stocked with the rules and metaphors of sports.

How about this one? "Happy is the man whose pig has no avatar." That means that a man is happy if his pig is not a god in disguise. If a man is of a faith that believes gods can reside in pigs, then he might be happy to know that his pig is not so inhabited. On the other hand, if he likes having a god about, he should be happy to have one in his sty. Or it might have nothing to do with his happiness, one way or another. So that one is a winner.

But there are troubles with this one: "He who pulls the lavatory chain during an earthquake does not blame the plumber if the house falls down." Granted, it sounds both profound and meaningless. But actually it shines with truth, a truth so universally recognized that it no doubt has been enunciated in every language. One of the oldest mentions is found in the lines of Fred Aesopulous, the legendary Greek shepherd-poet (c. 423 B.C.): "If the wine is green, do not blame the sheep." (This has also been translated as "do not blame your wife," but that is doubtful.) It means, of course, that one must not blame adversity on the wrong thing. Its best-known expression is in Shakespeare's *Julius Caesar:* "The fault, dear Brutus, is not in our stars, but in ourselves. . . ."

Knowing the pitfalls—especially the danger that one may unwittingly reveal some shy truth—I offer to the *New Statesman* as my own entry the following: "A baseball game is not won until it's lost."

I'm not sure that's a first, though; it sounds a little to me like Tommy Lasorda, the inspirational manager of the Los Angeles Dodgers, and I'm also afraid it has some truth in it.

After reading my mail, I am about persuaded that there is no such thing as a meaningless proverb.

Evidently, the English language is so rich that no one can put half a dozen words together in the form of a proverb without expressing some truth, however false. This can be formulated as "Everything makes sense." And I defy anyone to disprove that it isn't true.

For example, I observed that a baseball game is not won until it's lost, which at first glance might seem meaningless. Not only does it make sense—I wasn't even the first one to say it.

"Surely," writes Bryce Martin of Bakersfield, "you, an ex-sportswriter, know that Yogi Berra stated the case as succinctly as ever can be when he uttered the immortal: "It's not over until it's over."

And more recently, I am reminded, the same idea was expressed by the coach of a basketball team during a playoff game as: "The opera ain't over till the fat lady sings." This same proverb, in exactly those words, turned up more than once during that turnabout series between the Dodgers and the Expos in 1981, and no doubt will be heard again in seasons to come.

I am even more chagrined, as an ex-sportswriter, over a loophole in my football proverb: "Any gain is better than an incompletion."

"Try telling that to any NFL quarterback," writes Marv Wolf, "when their team is a few points behind and the clock has run down to less than two minutes. Would these paragons of the pass then opt for three or four yards on the ground instead of an incompletion? Not likely, because the time they lose is more precious than the ground they gain. The incompletion, especially if it is thrown out-of-bounds, is more to be desired than the time-consuming running play that eats at the sands of time. As you well know."

To those who have no interest in sports I apologize for these arcane digressions, but of course sports is merely the metaphor through which universal truths may be expressed—sometimes poetically—and that is what has happened here. Wolf's point is impeccable.

I said that "One man's catch is another man's wicket" was obviously related to the game of cricket, and consequently beyond the understanding of the American mind. That I was right is proved by Eric Heath of Tarzana. "The bowler (pitcher)," he explains, "bowls the ball. The batsman (let's say Casey) strikes the ball and before it touches the ground a fieldsman catches it. Casey is out, and it is the bowler's wicket: i.e., he got a man out (with an assist from the fielder)."

I get it, but it certainly isn't the sort of fair play one expects from the British. Why should the bowler get the fieldsman's wicket?

Fred McBryde of Arleta writes that he dreamed an apparently meaningless proverb one night in Korea in 1955 when he was in the Army: "If the string is long the pig is late." When he awoke he wrote it down and puzzled over it for weeks, asking his buddies if they had any idea what it meant.

Only gradually did the proverb reveal its hidden power. "I have quoted it hundreds of times since then," McBryde says, "in situations where nothing else seems to fit. The reactions I receive vary from blank questioning stares to total agreement with unquestioned truth. If the latter, I am usually embarrassed because the other person is obviously a fool for agreeing with a saying that is meaningless, or I am a fool for failing to recognize the basic truth of the statement that I just made."

Numerous readers have offered what they suppose are meaningless proverbs, only to add weight to my own. ("Everything makes sense.") For example: "Seen from the inside, the outside approaches infinity"—Douglas A. Russell, La Canada.

"You can drive a horse to drink, but you can't make him water"—Jeff Williamson, Sherman Oaks.

"Underweight people die more frequently than people of moderate weight"—quoted from the *Los Angeles Times* by Ed Shoaff, La Canada.

"Remember, we're all in this alone"—Lily Tomlin, according to Shoaff.

Several readers express sympathy with my confession that I have never understood what existentialism is. Others have sent me explanations that leave me more confused than I was before.

However, Herman Quick, a Renaissance man who taught for twenty years at Fairfax High, recalls a story that is held by authentic existentialists to be a luminous expression of their philosophy. In the men's room at Chasen's, it goes, someone wrote "To be or not to be—Hamlet." The next day someone added "To do is to be—Jean-Paul Sartre." The next day someone added "To be is to do—Albert Camus." The next day someone added "Do be do be do—Frank Sinatra."

"Now that," says Quick, "is existentialism, no matter what any other SOB tells you."

I have heard that story told of several other restaurants, so perhaps it's apocryphal. But it's as good an explanation of existentialism as I know. The only other one that makes sense is "If the string is long, the pig is late."

GOODBYE IS FOREVER

*Thank God
Shakespeare was a poet.*

Psychology, once thought to be the private concern of cranky old men with unkempt beards and impenetrable accents, has become almost as popular in America as tennis.

On every campus, teachers and students are prying into the nature and quirks of the human animal, trying to find out how we act and why. There is no closet of the human mind whose door we have not opened, looking in with our little flashlights. But today's researchers are not so much concerned with our aberrations, the sort of thing that delighted the likes of Krafft-Ebing; the focus today is on our everyday fears and myths, our likes and dislikes, the way we are.

Do blondes have more fun? Are the rich happier? Is it better for a girl to be pretty? Are football players braver? Is the sex revolution a success?

Until now we learned what we knew about human behavior from novelists, poets, old wives and our own observations. And as far as I can tell, today's elaborate inquiries, conducted with the assistance of computers, laboratory experiment and scientific polls, have pretty well demonstrated that the novelists, poets and old wives were usually right.

A few years ago a team at UCLA conducted experiments to find out if those objects we call "conversation pieces" actually stimulate conversation. What they found out, naturally, was that it depends on the conversation piece and the people it is meant to stimulate. We didn't need a psychologist to tell us that a live python would stimulate more conversation at a cocktail party than a Zippo lighter, unless of course the people at the party were natives of the Ecuadorian jungle, in which case it might be the Zippo.

In the 1970s three professors at Purdue conducted experiments to prove their theory that it is hard for people to end an interview, to actually get up and leave. The professors—Knapp, Hart and Friedrich—hired eighty students to interview other students or professors who weren't in on the experiment. Even though the hired students were to be paid more for quicker goodbyes, they couldn't end the interviews abruptly.

Evidently a person who ends a conversation abruptly is thought rude or arrogant, so we use a lot of what the professors call terminal indicators. "Most people wish to avoid unpleasantness, so they follow a little ritual to prepare themselves for the shock of parting, using up to fourteen types of words or phrases designed to reassure the 'partee' that the tête-à-tête is not being terminated, only interrupted."

It isn't that we don't know how to end a conversation abruptly. Any visitor who wants to depart needs only to look at his wristwatch, exclaim "Good heavens!" jump to his feet, extend a hand, say how rude he has been to stay so long, move toward the door, smile sincerely, say "Thank you and goodbye," and leave.

If the person wishing to end the interview happens to be the host, the routine is only slightly different. He too looks at his watch, but his reaction must be stronger. "Good God!" he whispers, clapping a hand to his forehead and looking absolutely stricken. He jumps to his feet, snatches his coat off a hanger and dashes for the exit, suddenly remembers his guest, turns, says "Please forgive me," checks his watch again, says "Let's get together for lunch sometime," and flees.

What Professors Knapp, Hart and Friedrich found out, though, is that most of us simply can't bring ourselves to act that way. We'd rather waste each other's time than seem rude or arrogant.

I only wish the professors had extended their experiments to the question of ending a conversation between two women saying goodbye in an open doorway, after a social evening. My own experience is that the only way to terminate such a conversation is to shut the door between the women, with force if necessary, leaving one inside and the other outside.

"Oh, fie!" writes Betty McElwain in response to my remarks on women and goodbyes. "Such male pigism, and coming from you. . . . At least I read William Buckley warily, but you I have read trustingly, knowing that your wife was not really expected to carry out all those trash barrels."

And from Donald Getz of San Diego: "The only lengthier goodbyes than those said by two women in an open doorway are those said by two men, one behind the wheel of an automobile and the other on the outside. In my experience there is no way to terminate such a conversation short of calling a tow truck and having the auto towed away with the driver inside."

I supposed it was inevitable that my observation should be misinterpreted by some as sexist, when it was just the opposite—an observation that reflected my constant awareness of the devices women are obliged to adopt in a male-dominated society.

My point, of course, was that women talk in the doorway, after the men have said goodbye, because up until that moment they have been either busy in the kitchen or conversationally shut out.

That this is no longer as true as it used to be, I will happily concede. The fruits of liberation are as evident in the living room as in the marketplace. A woman who demands recognition as a whole person, not merely a married groupie, is not content to sit with folded arms, stifling yawns, while her husband holds forth on the merits of the zone defense as against the one-on-one, or whether the Rams are passing too much on first down. (I think they are.)

No one can deny, though, that in many households this situation prevails today. The conversation isn't always about football. Sometimes it's baseball or the Middle East, or the price of gold. But in any case it's a subject that men traditionally regard as their own, although one almost never hears any of them say anything interesting or intelligent about it.

Sooner or later, as these know-it-alls drone on, interrupted only by an occasional pit stop at the bar, the women will quietly peel off, like birds that can't keep up with the formation, and begin talking to each other, keeping their voices down so as not to intrude on the torrents of hogwash from their mates.

Unless I actually have the floor myself, I often try to eavesdrop on these female asides, since they are almost always earthier, wittier and better informed than the mainstream conversation. They tend to be episodic, however, as one no sooner gets under way than a husband will yank his wife back to attention by asking her to fix him a drink or by some pretense of letting her into the general conversation.

"I believe Alice will agree with me on that," he will say. "Right, dear? Don't you think the NFL ought to adopt the two-point conversion option?"

So it is only at the end of the evening, when the men have emptied themselves of every last platitude and are flatulent and sleepy, that the women have a chance to exchange a few words at all. This they do in the doorway while their husbands drag themselves off to car and bedroom, each muttering to himself about what an idiot the other is.

That my sympathy in these situations is with the women should now be clear enough. I will be happy to see women get out of the doorway and into the conversation.

As for my own wife, she no longer prolongs our social evenings by talking in the doorway. In fact she has a very clever little ruse for bringing them to a sudden end.

"Well, if you'll excuse me," she says at midnight, "I have to put the trash barrels out in the morning."

Robert D. Kully, professor of speech communication at California State University, Los Angeles, has sent me a copy of *The Rhetoric of Goodbyes: Verbal and Nonverbal Correlatives of Human Leave-taking*, by Professor Gustav W. Friedrich of Purdue.

The paper is seventeen pages long, much of it in small type, and is naturally couched in scientific language—which could hardly be avoided, I suppose, since it is signed not only by Professor Friedrich but also by Professors Knapp, Hart and Shulman.

It is a fascinating study, this dissection of that common ritual of leave-taking. But I'm as fascinated by its language as by its findings. The four professors cite Ervin Goffman's suggestion that "greetings mark a transition to increased access, and farewells to a state of decreased access." (I think this means that when you say hello to a person you expect to be with him a while, and when you say goodbye you don't.)

"Perhaps," the professors observe, "this anticipation of lack of access is one of the factors that contributes to some of the difficulty that many of us have experienced in taking leave." (It's hard to say goodbye because you aren't going to be seeing the person for a while.)

Thus, they point out, "many of the behaviors associated with leave-taking are attempts to say, 'Yes, communicative access will be denied us for a while, but you should not perceive my leave-taking as threatening the end of our relationship.'"

But at cocktail parties, they observe, people don't say goodbye or farewell, or any of the words that suggest a long period of inaccessibility. "Cocktail parties provide a setting in which the probability of multiple encounters with the same person are generally increased. Thus, when short-term inaccessibility is anticipated, one finds various abbrevitaed forms of leave-taking being used—'Pardon me' or a 'knowing' touch on the arm."

I don't know. At the cocktail parties I go to the only way to escape from a one-on-one situation is to say, "My God, your drink is empty," snatch his or her glass and make for the bar, where one is safe until the next multiple encounter.

The professors have evidently been to one of those dreadful farewell parties where the guest of honor is got rid of at last, usually in no condition to depart, and then comes back to get his gloves or his wife, or whatever it is he's forgotten. They call these dismal occurrences "failed departures."

I recall a perfect example of a failed departure. It was years ago, a joyous wedding in the Hollywood Hills. The bride and bridegroom, after cake and champagne and many kisses and farewells, at last left in the bridegroom's father's Hudson, after which the guests at once settled into serious partying. Twenty minutes later, as the newlyweds sped south over the Pacific Coast Highway, the bride cried, "Oh, golly, I forgot my purse!" Having no wish to take part in a failed departure, the bridegroom wouldn't have gone back, but the honeymoon money was in the purse.

I remember the incident vividly, having been the bridegroom.

As fascinating as I found the Purdue report, thank God Shakespeare was a poet, not a behavioral scientist, or we might have had this:

JULIET: Good night, good night!
ROMEO: Yes, communicative access will be denied us for a while, but you should not perceive leave-taking as threatening the end of our relationship.

It is no reflection on the work of Professor Friedrich and his friends that it goes, instead, like this:

JULIET: Good night, good night!
ROMEO: Parting is such sweet sorrow
That I shall say good night
till it be morrow.

THE ICEBOX GOETH

Ever hear of snuggies?
Streetcars? BVDs?

We have lamented the passing from American life of certain sounds, such as the huff of steam locomotives and the cries of street vendors, and certain smells, such as the smell of leaves burning in the street, all of which produce a powerful nostalgia in those who remember them.

But words may also become outmoded, I am reminded by a reader, Roslyn Gaines, and words too have a nostalgic effect on people for whom they once were a part of everyday living.

Mrs. Gaines has been keeping a list of such words, among them: *icebox, slacks* (for ladies), *undertaker, galoshes, grocery store, rumpus room, pocketbook, gear shift* and *skyscraper.*

It's true. As our language accumulates new words— at a rate so fast the dictionaries can't keep up—it is inevitable that some of the old words that have served us well are discarded, or wither away from lack of use. They hang in the dictionary like dead leaves on a tree;

nobody bothers to blow them away. In time they simply fall, unheard, unseen, unmourned.

Let us mourn a little. Mrs. Gaines strikes home when she lists *icebox* among outdated words. Not only do I remember when we all had iceboxes in the house, and were dependent on the daily delivery by the man we called by a name that is also gone (the iceman), I still call it the icebox—even though it operates on electricity and never has enough ice in it for more than half a dozen highballs.

The word *icebox* is simple, graphic and evocative. How did we get conned out of *icebox* and into *refrigerator*? No doubt that sesquipedalian monster was dropped on us by the manufacturers of the first electric iceboxes, which came along when we were all enamored of the new technology and every new product, from aspirin tablets to iceboxes, had to have a name that sounded scientific.

I'm not so sure about some of Mrs. Gaines's other nominations. *Slacks,* evidently, has been ousted by pants in the women's-wear world, but exactly why that is I am unable to guess; a symptom, perhaps of the vogue for unisex?

The word *undertaker* is gone, of course, buried by the morticians in the name of euphemism, just as *mortician* itself has given way to *funeral director*, yet a newer euphemism, and that too will be dropped once people find out that a funeral director is really an undertaker in linguistic disguise.

Grocery store is almost gone, or at least is rare enough to sound quaint. I live in an old section of town where we still have one or two grocery stores, Ma and Pa institutions where children still get a sack of gumdrops when their parents pay the bill. But even these anachronisms like to call themselves *little supermarkets*, and everything they sell is hermetically sealed in plastic, so we are denied the aroma of coffee, pickles, licorice and spices that made the old grocery store a haven of sensuous delights.

The *gear shift* has been replaced not only as a word but, in most American cars, as a fact. We all have automatic transmissions now, at least those of us who still call refrigerators iceboxes. And among those who still enjoy a sense of mastery over their cars, the gear shift is a stick.

Rumpus room seems to have become *family room*, I gather from the classified ads; *skyscrapers* are turning into *high-rises*, and *movies* into *films*.

My own list would include *croon* and *crooner*. Here is a word that defined a whole generation of idols. Then suddenly, overnight, those idols were buried under an avalanche of rock set loose by a group of upstarts out of Liverpool, who not only didn't croon, but sang in a way to wake the dead, or at least a generation of sleeping teen-agers.

What ever happened to the *slow ball*? I have listened to Vin Scully for years without hearing a single reference to the pitch that once made fastball pitchers doubly dangerous and turned good batters into clowns. We have *curves* and *sliders* and *change-ups*. But where is the *slow ball*? Did pitchers give it up? Was it only a myth? Or is the *change-up* only a *slow ball* by another name?

Another word that has vanished, at least from my hearing, is *marcel*. I miss it. *Marcel* is a very pretty word, and it reminds me of my mother. She was always in need of one, or said she was. What she would be in need of today, I suppose, would be a permanent. But the frizzled hairdos of the 20s have had a comeback, and so has the hot curling iron, my wife tells me, and maybe the marcel.

I don't know what to say about *galoshes*. I have lived all my life in California and Hawaii, and I never owned a pair of galoshes. To me, galoshes are comical accoutrements, and I always think of a man in galoshes as galumphing, instead of walking.

"Did you ever hear of *snuggies?*" asks Edith Zittler. "Any female who waited for streetcars and buses in sub-zero weather some years back will know. They were short woolen pants under the girdle or over the girdle or ... next to the skin."

Streetcars? Girdle?

"And when was the last time," asks Lou Rosen of San Diego, "you heard someone mention their *BVDs?* I can't even remember what the letters stood for."

I wore them, and I recall that just the mention of BVDs in polite company was good for a snicker. (The name comes from Bradley, Voorhees and Day, founders of B.V.D. Co., New York City.)

"As for *galoshes,*" writes Grace Wood of San Gabriel, who came here from the East in 1922, "I have worn those cloth galoshes with metal fasteners, which we left open to flap as we walked (1921). I have heard that this is how the word *flapper* originated."

Flapper?

V. R. Chapman of Laguna Hills out of Nebraska, has jettisoned his thermal underwear, fur cap, fur-lined gloves and woolen mufflers, but he still has his galoshes. "I wear them when I wash the car with the hose. That way my feet come out dry—a great reward."

Tom Alexander of Laguna Beach comes up with *lead pencil, fountain pen* and *soda fountain,* among others, and *crackerjack,* meaning real good.

I don't know. The ballpoint pen, though nearly universal now, hasn't entirely displaced the lead pencil and the fountain pen. As for the soda fountain, I think it still exists in Hollywood—or where would tomorrow's Lana Turners be discovered?

Claire Estelle still says icebox and Victrola, but deplores the loss of two words that have not died, but been kidnaped and sold into prostitution.

"Let us consider *swing,*" she mourns. "As its usage moved outward to include (besides its original concept of back and forth motion) a style of music and dance, I was able to absorb this, since I danced swing dances to swing music. I cut a rug, so to speak. As the root word evolved into *swinger,* I was able to follow and use the word properly to describe a devil-may-care bon vivant, an insouciant life of the party. But now I must be very, very careful that I do not use the word as defined above, because the subsequent mutation shifted the meaning into an uncomfortably different realm.

"But I think the word I miss the most in its old form," she adds, "is *gay.* The dictionary speaks of merriment and excitement. I would add to that froth, ebullience and light-hearted spontaneity. What a pity that another word wasn't chosen ... for people whose personal fulfillment differs from the conventional."

I don't mind so much the evolution of *swing* and *swinger,* as I never could cut a rug; but without resenting those who have appropriated it, I do miss *gay.* As rich as our languge is, it has no really good substitute for *gay.*

A reader who doesn't want her name mentioned (she blushes easily) points out the quiet, almost unnoticed disappearance of a word that not long ago was a part of every mixed-company conversation—*risqué.* Not only has the word itself disappeared, but also the kind of story or remark it defined. "Sadly," she says, "no such thing exists anymore. So sorry. Unforbidden things are really not as much fun (as Huxley enlarged upon)."

Quite. And gone with *risqué* is its companion, the *double entendre.* Now that everything is permitted to hang out, as we say, and unrestrained speech is regarded as liberating and healthful, there is no point in trying to turn out one of those clever conversational coins that are gold on one side and blue on the other.

Come to think of it, is there such a word as *blush* anymore?

In our passion for the new we have thrown out some very good things. Let's have the marcel back, and the slow ball, and running boards.

I will leave the last word to an old acquaintance of mine, Easy Sloman, who happens to have the best name I have ever heard.

"Nostalgia," says Easy, "just isn't what it used to be."

A LUPANAR IS NOT A HOME

"Your readers may become textual perverts."

Although it is never my practice to use obscure words merely to impress or intimidate, I will not shy away from what I think is the *right* word, however intimidating it may be; and of course I have no choice when the word occurs in quoted matter.

Thus I have received a few inquiries from readers who came across the word *lupanars* and not only didn't know what it meant but couldn't find it in their dictionaries and couldn't puzzle it out from the text.

The word was used by Judge Ronald E. Swearinger of the Los Angeles Superior Court, in a letter reminiscing about his youthful days as an iceman in Vallejo, a lusty watefront town on San Pablo Bay north of San Francisco.

"My route used to include several lupanars," he said, "where I was always treated with abundant generosity, including Lucullan breakfasts with the proprietresses and the habitues, all of whom thought

I was too skinny for a sixteen-year-old kid. Such mornings I would eat as many as five breakfasts and was often encouraged to say the blessing, or to participate in the prayer meeting."

Among those who were stumped by *lupanars* was Katherine Geffine of Lakewood, Ohio. "I was a weekend guest in Fullerton," she writes, and "mine host's only dictionary *(The World Book)* did not contain your word. So I could only imagine from my limited Latin a root-like noun meaning wolfish (feminine gender), or even a unique skin disorder.

When she returned to the guest ranch where she sojourns for half of every year, she went to look the word up in the ranch dictionary. "I found to my dismay that their library provides only a tattered volume which could be one of Noah Webster's original editions. A trip to the local library is now in order."

Lael Littke of Pasadena had no more success though she had a better dictionary. "My eyes traveled smoothly down the page until they wrecked on *lupanars.* I quickly heaved my hernia edition of the *Random House Dictionary of the English Language* over to the light and turned to the proper page, which listed *luny, Lin Yu,* and *lupe.* No *lupanar.*

"I'm in the dark as to what a lupanar is. Do you know? Or are you just taking the word of a man who unof the Los Angeles Superior Court? I really would like to know. It's a word I haven't been introduced to, even edly has impeccable credentials, being a judge though I usually pass the 'Increase Your Word Power' tests in *Reader's Digest.*"

I am not embarrassed to confess that the word was a stranger to me, too, but I am surprised that Mrs.

Geffine and Mrs. Littke, both of whom obviously are women of intelligence and curiosity, failed to arrive at the probable meaning of the word by textual inference.

This is the process by which a person encountering an unfamiliar word, usually in speech, can guess its definition from an analysis of the text in which it occurs. In somewhat this way, I believe, astronomers are able to posit the presence of heavenly objects which they cannot actually see.

No matter how large our vocabularies, most of the words we know have been learned by this process of textual inference, and not by consulting a dictionary. I imagine there are people with rather large vocabularies who have never opened a dictionary in their lives.

Thus, though I have half a dozen good dictionaries at hand, it was a matter of pride with me to flesh out the meaning of Judge Swearinger's word by this method. Actually, it was rather easy, since the paragraph in which it occurred was rich in clues.

We have, to begin with, a place that requires ice; i.e., a place where people reside—a hostel. It is occupied by women, since we have the word proprietresses. We know that these proprietresses (a word, which, by the way, recalls the word prioresses, perhaps an earlier form) were abundantly generous. Food evidently was not taken in these places without a word of thanks to its Provider, and there was a regular period of general prayer.

I don't think anyone needs either a large vocabulary or a trip to Vallejo to guess that young Swearinger's lupanars were convents or nunneries, and that his proprietresses and habitués, i.e., persons wearing habits, were nuns. (Since there were several of these establishments on the young man's route, we may further infer that Vallejo was a very religious town in those days.)

In making this conclusion I might have been troubled by those Lucullan breakfasts, which seem out of place in a holy house, but a vow of poverty does not mean that one must starve. And it is probable that not only did his solicitous hostesses see that their skinny visitor got a working man's share of what was perhaps a modest meal, but his hunger and their generosity made it seem more Lucullan than it was.

I suppose now I will hear from readers who don't know what *Lucullan* means. I leave them to their inferences.

Not since I ruptured my disk have I received so many letters as I have in response to my definition, by textual inference, of the word *lupanar* (pronounced loo-PAY-n'r).

My textual inference that lupanars were nunneries or convents has brought comment ranging from lofty contempt to conspiratorial amusement, and included a number of philosophical or scholarly observations.

"Please see *Webster's New Collegiate Dictionary* for the word *lupanar*," writes Ruth S. Wise of Sherman Oaks. "You will find that this word comes from the Latin word *lupa*, meaning prostitute, literally she-wolf, and means brothel."

Others advise that *lupanar* also means brothel in French, Portuguese, Spanish and Italian—which it does.

"*Webster's New International Dictionary* (2nd edition) unmistakably defines *lupanars* as brothels," writes Christopher Mankiewicz, "not convents or nunneries. So much for your smug methodology!"

"While there may well have been a convent (or two) in Vallejo," writes Barbara Dower, "I am more inclined to infer that the good Judge Swearinger was talking about another kind of house."

"Your handling of the word *lupanar* was very delicate," writes James A. Scott of Ontario, "but are you not going to relieve the curiosity of your philologist readers?"

"My conclusion," writes Christina Witsberger of Santa Monica, "is that you are either trying to put one over on your readers, have never been to Vallejo, or are incredibly naive."

"Your tongue-in-cheek pursuit of *lupanars* through contextual clues had me grinning," writes Bill Mitchell of Downey. "You made a point which I hope was not lost on your readers: namely, that though context is important, there are times when nothing but the dictionary will do. Beautiful!"

"As a native of Vallejo (lo that many years ago)," writes Lolita E. Griffin of Manhattan Beach, "I sure don't remember an overabundance of nunneries. I do remember my mother hustling me past certain blocks of that swinging town, and I was not to look at those fancy-dressed ladies. Nuns? No way, José!"

"Lupanar or nunnery, Lucullan or not," writes G. Merle Bergman, "what I marvel at is how the boy Swearinger ever got this ice delivered, what with five breakfasts in one morning plus five prayer meetings."

"Possibly at the same time," writes Pete Pringle of Balboa Island, "I carried the Portsmouth (N.H.) morning paper to many a similar establishment, as sailors dashed down the stoops at dawn to catch the liberty boat to the naval yard at Kittery, Maine, across the Piscataqua River. But I was given naught but sweet smiles from kimono-clad subscribers and went on my way with only the fragrance of frying bacon and baking johnny cake for my hunger. Plus fading but exotic perfumes, probably gifts of customers just back with the fleet from the south of France or Naples."

Finally, for those serious philologist readers, perhaps I should conclude this diversion with an etymological note from the poet, scholar and fabulist Robert Nathan: "A lupanar was a Roman brothel during the Flavian period. You will find it in the Fourth Book of *In Medias Res Memorialissimi* by Heliotropus, a journeyman writer of travel guides, born in Cyprus but Romanized during the reign of Caligula. The word does not evolve from *lupe*, or wolf, but from the Visigoth *lumpen*, to dance and to enjoy oneself."

Now for a good Lucullan breakfast.

TRUTH SHINES THROUGH

"Man hit by automobile— speaks broken English."

You wouldn't think an insurance company would laugh at claims that are likely to cost it money, but sometimes the language people use in filing claims is more severely fractured than the broken legs they describe.

Recently the Prudential Insurance Company's employee newspaper, *Who's News,* regaled 2,400 people who work in the home office by publishing a few gems from claims filed by policyholders.

That old standby, the malapropism, turns out to be in good health. Here it is, for example, in the description of an unusual assault: "My wooden leg was broken. A man hit me with a ranch."

The company took that word to mean "wrench." But I don't know. When a cowboy falls off his horse and breaks his wooden leg he might very well think he's been hit by a ranch.

"While sitting in a tavern," wrote another claimant, "someone hit my nose from behind." And another: "While dancing in the Navy someone stepped on my hand."

Both of these victims sound as if someone might have hit them with the floor. It's the type of accident I've seen more than once, having frequented a few taverns with aggressive floors.

Some of the statements were models of vivid condensation. "An airplane hit the house and came in."

A victim of what evidently was rheumatic fever described himself as having been stricken by "romantic flavor." There was also a victim of "romantic fervor," as picturesquely described in these few words: "While waving goodnight to a friend, I fell out of a two-story window."

Perhaps less romantic but no less picturesque was the misadventure of a virtuous young lady, I presume, who reported, "my downfall occurred on the stairway."

Sometimes the claims are models of candor: "Put tire patch on Playtex girdle," reported one woman, "and it caused infection on right thigh." I'm not an adjuster, of course, but it seems to me this woman has a claim against the people who made the tire patch, as well as Prudential.

I certainly can sympathize with the fellow who reported, "Hernia, from pulling a cork out of a bottle." Prudential might do well to give each of its policyholders a good corkscrew. One hernia is worth a thousand corkscrews.

Most of the claims, illiterate or not, have the ring of truth. "I dislocated my shoulder swatting a fly." It happens that I've never dislocated a shoulder at this sport, but I have knocked over two table lamps and several highballs and skinned an elbow.

No one who has ever been trapped at a live rock concert can have the slightest doubt of this claim: "Headaches and earaches caused by my guitar." That person has suffered enough, without being accused of misspelling catarrh.

And so has the person who complained: "I wake up unconscious."

One victim described graphically an experience most of us have had: "Getting on a bus, the driver started before I was all on."

Influenza threw several claimants. One reported "a light case of severe flu," which is perfectly accurate, if you've ever had it. Another complained of "flue with a small touch of ammonia." I've heard of taking a touch of ammonia for a hangover, but not for the flue.

Funny as they may be, these efforts have one common strength. We know what they mean. They demonstrate the marvelous clarity and vigor of our language in the service of people who know what they're talking about and are telling the truth.

If only our income tax laws were as clear; and yes, our insurance policies, maybe we wouldn't wake up unconscious so often.

Judge Mario L. Clinco, of the Superior Court in Santa Monica, has a similar list he's been collecting for years. Judge Clinco's gems are mostly excerpts from reports filed by social service workers investigating applicants for public assistance.

Like the claims of the policyholders, they may be fraught with malapropisms and unintended double meanings, but their truth shines through.

Imagine the surprise of the social worker who

walked into this situation: "Woman and house neat but bare."

And the case of the inadequate father: "Milk needed for the baby and father unable to supply it."

It is proof of the vitality and perversity of humor that all these laughs are derived from human misery. Even as we laugh, we can see all too vividly the bleak faces and squalid rooms.

"Woman in a quarry—too old to work, too young for a pension."

They are all in a quarry, like Sisyphus of Greek mythology, who was condemned to spend eternity pushing a huge stone up a mountain, only to have it roll back every day.

"Woman has no job to be mentioned."

"Woman is saving up for an illness."

Often it seems possible that there might be some truth in the unintended side of the double meaning. "Couple breaking up home—friends helping." "Family's savings all used up—relatives have helped."

The husband is often invisible, except in the evidence of his progeny. "Applicant and wife are illegally separated." "Saw mother and child, evidence of father." "Man aggressive—has nine children." "Woman still owes $45 for a funeral she had recently." (If the funeral was for a man like that aggressive husband, it was a bargain.)

Some of these people haven't always been down and out. "Until a year ago this applicant delivered ice and was a man of affairs." "These people are extremely cultured. Something should be done about their condition." "Applicant is a lady and hardly knows what it is all about." "Good type American family—appear refined, but intelligent."

Sometimes neighbors are no more trustworthy than relatives. "Applicant's wife is making little garments through the kindness of a neighbor." "Applicant and family got $15 from neighbors for moving from former address."

There is evidence here and there of the unflagging human spirit. "Mother is willing to struggle if given an opportunity." "Man recently had operation but is able to hold any position he assumes."

Some of the reports suggest utter destitution. "Applicant worked in children's underwear. Let out recently."

Many of these people, beaten down by circumstances, are understandably short on education. "Woman says husband has illness that sounds like arithmetic."

Perhaps no connection between two facts was intended here, but the idea is compelling: "Man hit by automobile—speaks broken English."

I phoned Judge Clinco to ask him how long he'd been collecting these rough pebbles and he said it dated from the 1940s, when he sat on a federal pension and compensation board in Philadelphia. But evidently three decades of social welfare haven't changed the picture much.

"I have one right here in front of me," the judge said. "This woman says, 'I have eight children—what are you going to do about it?'"

Judge Clinco didn't know what to do about the poor woman and I don't either.

WHEN YOU'RE SIXTY-FIVE

(What will they call you?)

Having reached an age at which the question is somewhat more than academic, I have been giving some thought to the following appeal from a reader, Phyllis Lewis:

"I write to ask if you can't do something about the nuts who think people at sixty-two and sixty-three are elderly. If that's old, what is my dad at eighty-nine?"

The same plea comes from Rosalie Higgs, who writes:

"We down here in Long Beach are getting mighty tired of saying aging persons ... senior citizens ... elderly.... If you can find a good term or word which has better connotations, that will be the real miracle. As you know, we have a large population of mostly older people and we need help."

"For some time," writes Bryan Aleksich, "I have been searching for an acceptable term that might replace senior citizens and similarly uncomfortable appellations applied to people who seem to somehow acquire a disability simply from having lived a long time, or just longer than others have—no matter how healthy and productive."

Aleksich notes that in France such people are called *troisième*, or third age, and thinks the term would work well here. Having no further explanation, I infer that *troisième* refers to the last third (more or less) of a person's lifetime: the part that comes after sixty, or perhaps sixty-five.

Troisième does have a softer sound than senior citizen, but perhaps that is only because it is new to our ears. Once it came into wide use, I imagine, it would become just as unsatisfactory as senior citizen. As soon as a euphemism's meaning is instantly understood, it is no longer a euphemism. No term that sets off old people as a class, I suspect, will ever be loved by them. For example, old people—which I have just used.

I'm not sure we'll ever find a better term for senior citizens. For one thing, people who may be thought of by others as senior citizens are far too different, one from another, to be categorized by a single phrase.

As distasteful as senior citizen may be to many senior citizens, it may be preferable to the several alternatives. Old folks was all right when the tone of America was set by Edgar A. Guest, but of course it won't do today. *Folks* don't live in spa-condominiums and drive RVs and spend more time in the air than geese. Elders sounds too biblical; seniors too collegiate; aging too meaningless (who isn't?); aged too aged; and old too old.

I have begun to take the problem more to heart

now that I have been called a senior citizen myself, or at least asked if I was one.

I first had this unnerving experience when my wife and I were in London. We were visiting Dr. Samuel Johnson's home, off Fleet Street, and we encountered a young woman who sat at a small desk on which a card said: Admission £1. I withdrew two pound-notes from my wallet and dropped them on the desk. The woman looked up at me uncertainly.

"Are you sixty-five?" she asked.

I was taken aback. "What?" The question seemed impertinent, at best, and I certainly couldn't imagine what had made her think I might be.

She explained: Persons over sixty-five were admitted at half-fee, and since I had only given her a pound-note for the two of us, she thought we were of that vintage, a conclusion that was not, she assured us, borne out by our youthful looks.

It turned out to be a simple misunderstanding. The two pound-notes I had dropped on the table were stuck together, so that they appeared to be only one.

I had managed to put the incident out of mind until just the other night when my wife and I went to a movie on Hollywood Boulevard and the girl in the box office said, "Are you senior citizens?"

She must have noticed my dismay. She giggled. "I just thought," she said, "well, it's half-price if you're senior citizens."

"I'm afraid we're not," I said, realizing that I didn't mind admitting my age, but I couldn't stand being called a senior citizen—not even to save a couple of dollars. I wasn't ready yet for that.

Tens of thousands of us are becoming senior citizens every day, and before long the generation that didn't trust anybody over thirty will be twice that. What will they want their children to call them?

Often, when we need a new word, we find we already have it, hidden away in slightly different form. We already have words to differentiate between people of more than sixty years, by decades; sexagenarian for those in their sixties; septuagenarian, seventies; octogenarian, eighties; nonagenarian, nineties; and centenarian, hundreds. Thus, if we call a person a nonagenarian we know we are not talking about a senior citizen in his sixties.

Of course these six-syllable words are too long and too Latin to be loved. So I suggest trimming them down to catchy abbreviations. Why not sexos for sixty-year-olds, septos for seventy-year-olds, and so on—octos, nonos and centos?

These words are short, plain, easy to say and easy to remember. They're as convenient as nickels and dimes, and would soon become as familiar and as easy to handle.

And if there were a need for referring to senior citizens as a group—encompassing all ages over sixty—what's wrong with genarians? In other words, a man of eighty-two is a genarian, but more specifically, an octo.

If anyone thinks these suggestions are frivolous or unkind, I point out that I have recently become a sexo myself, and I rather like the sound of it.

It goes especially well with Irish whisky.

I am not innocent enough to have supposed that my suggestion would be widely adopted, but the response seems to indicate that most senior citizens themselves aren't happy with senior citizen.

"As one sexo to another," writes Maxwell H. Smith, "welcome to the genarian group, of which I have been a member for six years. I think your idea is superb. It should be adopted."

"I too am approaching the age of sexo," writes Shirley Martin of Reseda, "and for the first time I'm looking forward to being admitted into that special category. Since I am presently embarking on a whole new mode of life, I am not particularly anxious to be referred to as a senior citizen who could be sixty or ninety, full of life or vegetating. It does appeal to me to be referred to as a sexo. I, too, rather like the sound of it."

"Sexo is a great term," writes Mary Aguilar of Laguna Hills. "Actually, it should be the general classification for all those past sixty. Everyone knows what sex is, but let the younger ones conjecture what the *o* stands for. Is it often, occasional, omitted, ominous, ouch, over, obsolete or outstanding?"

But others, and they may be right, aren't jumping on the sexo wagon.

"I see no need for a word to set persons apart from others according to age," writes Mark Nichols. "Specific is OK—ten-year-old, ninety-four-year-old—but fifty-two or fifty-four doesn't mean a lot unless the guy has just been named chairman of the board of General Electric. Orson Welles peaked at twenty-four, Verdi in his eighties, and sexo Smitho sure dreams of doing something better than he has ever done before."

"It isn't the word for the over-sixties that is the problem," writes Alice Bock of Panorama City. "It's the practice of putting such a large and varied group of individual human beings into a single category that's the problem. Once we pass that fateful birthday (sixty or sixty-five), do we stop being the unique persons we were before? Of course not."

"I too find the term senior citizen offensive," writes Rosemary McDonald of Pasadena, "perhaps because it makes me feel we are giving a condescending pat on the back. . . . Perhaps this subject is depressing to me because I am fast reaching the time when I may be referred to by one of these terms. I do hope someone will come up with a term that has flamboyancy and dignity before I reach that point."

But senior citizen is not without its friends.

"Please don't mess around with the nice title senior citizens," says Dolores Z. Cascales of Woodland Hills. "I am more than satisfied with the title we have, especially when I step up and buy a $4 ticket to a movie, and read on the sign: Senior Citizens $2.50."

Yet others see no need for a modern coinage when ancient custom has already provided a word.

"I would rather be called an elder citizen than a sexo or an octo," writes Eric Egge of Balboa. "In spite of other connotations, elder denotes achievement and dignity. Septo and octo sound too much like rhino or dodo."

"I respectfully submit respected elders," writes Jim Hansen, "to borrow a term from many cultures. True, it does not fit everyone over a certain age, but it's a nice phraseology."

I might have survived these various winds and stayed with sexo and genarian. But it's a note from Robert Nathan that moves me to strike my colors.

"It's all very well for you to revel in the idea of yourself as a sexo," he says, "but I'm not at all pleased to see myself as an octo, which sounds like a small, furry, spidery animal clambering up and down trees. And I shall hate even more to be called a nono—or no no—with all that it implies.

"Why not an elder? Granted it's a bit biblical, but it does have a certain authority, and at the same time suggests that one is still spry (or sly) enough to peek through the bushes at Susannah."

All right. Elder is OK with me if it's OK with Susannah, and we still get a discount at the movies.

BELLES-LETTRES

"The pizza hut burned down and safeway got on fire."

There is much evidence that many children manage to get all the way into college without learning how to write a simple English sentence, so any scrap of evidence to the contrary is encouraging.

I am grateful to have been allowed to copy and publish a letter a co-worker of mine received recently from her six-year-old niece, Kathryn, a first-grader in Lincoln Nebraska. The letter follows, as written. (I have made no corrections except to add periods at the end of each sentence. Even this modest liberty may be presumptuous. There have been numerous experiments in this century, by writers of poetry and prose, in eliminating the period and other punctuation marks as distracting and unnecessary. However, I am too old a dog to learn that trick and if literary anarchy is what this child is really up to, I don't wish to encourage her at this point. She must learn to walk before she flies.)

Dear Aunt Betts:

I was underdog. My friend was a witch. I wish you could come here. Cynthia was a bientennial girl. Are fish are still alive. I have spelling tomorow. I have easy work. My mom went to Omaha until 9:00. I have 28 candy bars 13 pieces of gum. I have lots of candy from Halloween.

Today we went to the Hilton and they had spaghetti and meat balls. They had coconut cake with a strawberry on top. In reading we are the highest one. In math we are on page 75. In reading we are on page 57. I ride on the bus to YMCA on Tuesday for gymnastics and swimming.

My teacher name is Mrs. Zieg. Cynthia rides her bike and I walk with friends. Are gym teacher is in the hospital. The pizza hut burned down and safeway got on fire. Today I went to Apple hill farm with my friend. Hope you had lots of fun on Halloween.

Love, Kathryn

There were several smudges on the paper, a sign of much erasing. But the writer doesn't live who has no need to edit and correct his work. Also, the reader may have noticed the spelling of *our* as *are*. However, it should be noted that such difficult words as *spaghetti, Halloween* and *gymnastics* are spelled correctly, and she came very close to getting *Bicentennial,* which isn't easy.

I should like to point out also that *tomorrow* happens to be misspelled in the sentence, "I have spelling tomorow," so we may hope that the very next day she learned how to spell it.

Those are trifles. The important thing is the author's simple, straightforward expository style, as lean and lucid as the early Hemingway. For example: "We went to the Hilton and they had spaghetti and meat balls." How reminiscent of those memoirs in which Hemingway was always telling us that they ate a fish at a little cafe on the Boulevard Saint Germain and the wine was cold and good and afterwards they went back to the hotel and ... oh, well, you know Hemingway.

As for hard news, this child passes it on with an economy of words and an emotional detachment that has marked the best reporting from the time of Thucydides. "The pizza hut burned down and safeway got on fire." There they are, the facts, boiled down to an irreducible minimum; yet the reader needs no more to make him see the Pizza Hut in flames, the fire engines clanging up to the smoking Safeway, the people running out.

Inevitably, as in even the best reporting, there are statements that call for elucidation. One is left hungering for more. "In math we are on page 75. In reading we are on page 57." These are flawless sentences. One wonders, though, just what page 75 in math means. Is the class into long division already, or fractions? And what are they reading on page 57?

I am also left wondering by the author's first sentence. "I was underdog." From what follows I guess that Kathryn went trick-or-treating on Halloween as an underdog. If so, I would certainly like to know more. How does a small girl dress as an underdog? Surely the representation of an abstract word like underdog would require ingenious costuming, and I would be happy to give 28 candy bars and 13 pieces of gum for a picture of Kathryn dressed up as one. She has also thrown away a provocative line, not explained, in the manner of Agatha Christie planting a clue that is to be recalled later in the story and revealed as critical. "I ride on the bus to YMCA on Tuesday for gymnastics and swimming." Could this mean that in Lincoln the YMCA is taking girls? That would be significant, I think, in contrast with the action of the Girl Scouts of America in excluding boys.

I am eager for my friend to receive her next letter. I hope to find out that the fish are still alive, and that Kathryn has corrected her ours and her tomorrows.

My French daughter-in-law also has a genius for writing the brief, graphic, expository note, and she is capable of adding a tone of drama. However, I sometimes find her messages ambiguous, perhaps because English is not her native language.

We were just about to leave the house to go out to dinner one evening when the phone rang, as it seems to do when you already have the front door open and the car keys in your hand. I went back into the kitchen to answer it.

"Mr. Smith? That is you?"

It was my daughter-in-law. I told her that indeed it was me (or I, if you please, but I'm sure I said me).

"I have wonderful news," she said with her usual exuberance. "Today I took both the children to the dentist and guess what? The dentist say their teeth are beautiful! They have *no* cavities!"

"That's wonderful," I said. "Just like in the commercials."

I knew why she had called me. She not only knew I would be pleased that my grandchildren had no cavities, but she wanted to crow just a bit, because I had often expressed my concern over the amount of candy and Coke she let them have. I try not to give advice in my family, but everybody is a nut about something, and my thing is sugar and teeth. I was congratulating her for this triumph when she interrupted:

"Mr. Smith I call you back my oven is on fire!"

At that point my wife recalled later, I said, "We're leaving—I'll call you when we get home." But subsequent events indicated that my daughter-in-law had already hung up and didn't hear me.

Anyone who has read any history about war knows that the greatest battles may turn on a late message, or even a message that arrives on time but is ambiguous, and is consequently misinterpreted. It was the breakdown of communications between Napoleon's infantry and cavalry—as well as the rain—that cost him the battle of Waterloo.

Families too, as well as armies, must often depend on hasty and imperfect messages for their coordinated functioning. No member of my family is more aware of this than I am, and it is my practice to study every note that is left for me, to make certain I know exactly what it means. Thus my confusion and anxiety on finding the following note when we returned from dining out that evening. It was written in my daughter-in-law's baroque scrawl, covering a full sheet of scratch paper, and had been fixed by a small magnet to the hood of the kitchen range, which is how we leave our messages.

Dear Mr. Smith,
We are glad you were not home. I called you
right back after we extinguished the fire in the
oven, but you did not answer so after keeping
calling you, I started to get scared maybe you
got a heart attack or something. We decided to
drive to your house just to be sure (everybody
was afraid to get in). Now we are just worried
that you decided to come to our house just to be
sure that we were all right. We are glad you are
alive and well.

Jacqueline

"If we weren't here," my wife said, "how do they
know you're alive and well?"

That bothered me too, but I was still having
trouble with the first sentence. "We are glad you
were not home." Certainly that is a strange message
to get from someone who has driven to your house
to see you.

I considered that sentence in the light of the later
one—"I started to get scared maybe you got a heart
attack or something . . . everybody was afraid to get
in." It was clear enough then. She was glad I wasn't
home because that was better than finding me home
but dead of a heart attack.

"They probably thought *I* wasn't home yet," my
wife said, "because this is my board meeting night.
They thought you were alone."

I began to see how they reasoned. She had told me
her oven was on fire and then hung up. When the
fire was out, she called me back, assuming I would
be waiting anxiously by the telephone. There was

no answer. I wouldn't have gone out, because I would be too worried about the fire. If I hadn't gone out, and wasn't answering the phone, I must have had an emergency of my own. A heart attack.

They had worried about that for a minute and then decided to drive over and find out what was wrong. They had found nobody home. Not believing I would have gone out casually without waiting for a report on the fire, they decided I must have rushed over to their house. They had then gone home but I wasn't there. Finally my wife and I had come home and found the note.

"You'd better phone," I said, "and explain."

The reason we had gone out without waiting to find out about the fire was that I assumed it was merely a hamburger or a soufflé that had caught fire, and there was really no great danger. I burn things all the time. But evidently the fire was more dangerous than that, and they somehow expected me to be more worried.

The critical factors were two unheard or unremembered parts of the conversation: I didn't remember her saying I'll call you back, though our son verified that she had; and of course she didn't hear me say "We're leaving—I'll call when we get home," because she had already hung up.

But all's well that ends well. Thank God their house didn't burn down and I didn't have a heart attack. The main thing, of course, is that the children have no cavities.

THE FRENCH CONNECTION

Who among us wants to lose his derrière?

Every few years the French establishment turns liverish again over the intrusion of American words into the French language. Americanisms, they fear, are defiling *la belle Francaise* the way hamburgers have defiled the French cuisine.

The French academicians can bear this plague only so long, apparently, and then they begin swishing the air and thrashing about, attempting to eradicate the offensive words like a man swatting at flies with a sword.

It was back in 1950, according to my personal file on this matter, that a French bureau called *L'Office du Vocabulaire Francais* warned that such Americanisms as *cover girl, holdup, knockout, pipeline, best-seller, blackout* and *striptease* were debasing the most glorious of man's achievements, the instrument of Molière, La Rochefoucauld and De Gaulle.

Then again in 1964, I find, this strange form of xenophobia flared up again, this time in a book called *Parlez-Vous Franglais?* It was an attack by a Professor René Etiemble of the Sorbonne, on those

Frenchmen and Frenchwomen who were addicted to the pernicious hybrid, French-English.

The professor cited 5,000 words that had already breached the Maginot Line of the French vocabulary to violate the language, like so many Huns let loose among the maidens of the provinces. Like Zola shouting *"J'accuse!"* the professor pointed a finger at *blue-jeans, best-seller, swank* and *weekend,* among others, and warned that if such barbarians weren't stopped at the English Channel, the language of France would be dead of the pox in forty years.

But it was not until thirteen years later that the French government itself called the great French bureaucracy to the colors. In 1977 it banned such Americanisms as *hit parade, tanker, zoning, flashback* and *one-man show* from official communications. Instead, appropriate substitutes must be used from a list of 350 patriotic French words recruited to stem the American tide.

The government not only ordered that the accredited French words be used in all official intercourse, but also strongly urged their use upon the general public—including, I imagine, the kind of people one used to find hanging out in Paris at Le Drug Store.

The French are entitled, surely, to keep their language clean of American litter if they can, but I hope we aren't stricken by the same fever in America, and try to purge our wonderful language of some of its Gallic ornaments.

I doubt if the French academy will find any French words as good as *blackout, holdup, striptease, gangster, cover girl* and *weekend.* They are gems of the American genius for inventing expressions of stunning rightness and indestructibility. As the French might say, we have *le knack* for *le mot juste.*

To understand the comic folly of the French government's campaign, we must try to imagine the American establishment publishing a list of taboo French words and their approved American substitutes.

Consider the plight of the Pentagon if it were under orders to strip Pentagonese of French words? What would become of our corporals and sergeants, our infantry, artillery and our cavalry? Worse, what would become of our generals? What would take the place of battle, victory and defeat? And what of war and peace?

What would we call blonds? Not lightheads, surely. Think up, quickly, a substitute for *divorcée*. What would we use instead of the handy French *brassière*? I can think of no other word or phrase for *brassière* that isn't either awkward or vulgar. And who among us wants to lose his *derrière*?

Surely we Americans don't begrudge the French the use of a small contingent of our words. We must remember that for three hundred years French was the official language of England, and it is said that half of Chaucer's vocabulary were words from France. We have survived. Why are the French so apoplectic about a few Americanisms that probably have a strain of French blood anyway?

As I see it, a little French American interchange adds to the *joie de vivre*. In dealing with the French, though, one never expects to have the last word. Or as the French would say, *le dernier cri*.

Every now and then, spurred by some wistful image of myself as a linguist, I take flight on the wings of French, only to be shot down—a sparrow among geese.

My French, in fact, is derived from one semester in college, which ended in my dropping out in disgrace; one week in France, where my French daughter-in-law's father poured half the wines of the Loire valley down me before I learned to say *assez*, enough; and an occasional letter from my daughter-in-law's sister, Nanette.

Whenever I am called upon to use a French word or phrase, I go directly to the French-English section in the back of my *Random House Dictionary of the English Languge,* or to my paperback copy of C. O. Sylvester Mawson's *Dictionary of Foreign Terms*—"More than 15,000 key phrases in over 50 foreign languages, for students, teachers and the everyday reader."

Finally, once I've worked out a phrase in French for myself, I check it with the highest authority immediately available—either my wife or my daughter-in-law. Before I acquired my daughter-in-law I had to rely exclusively on my wife, which often enough got me into difficulties. The French she learned at home is a provincial patois, and tends to make me look illiterate. My daughter-in-law, on the other hand, speaks the classic French of Tours, but her line is often busy and I can't get through when I need her.

This is what happened the other day when I asked the rhetorical question, "What would we use instead of the handy French brassière?"

I should have checked with my daughter-in-law. Among others who wrote to enlighten me was Maurice Rosset, a colleague and a Frenchman.

"You may truly say," he wrote, "that you Americans have really the knack of mot juste. Example: the word brassière. This French word is getting its proper usage only when spoken by English-speaking people. For the French brassière is a baby garment; a kind of T-shirt for the newly born and the very young. A bra in French is called soutien-gorge, or a throat-holder, which certainly it isn't. Why are the French so fond of euphemisms for the things they like to fondle?"

I have also heard from some women. "I am left with the definite impression," wrote Grace Brownridge of La Canada, "that you are confusing a French brassière with an American one! I shudder to think of the complications into which this error might lead you, and suggest that you have the French connections in your family confirm the fact that in French, a brassière is a baby's sacque, not a soutien-gorge."

The most graphic lesson, though, came in the form of a full-page advertisement, evidently torn from some French magazine, vintage 1968. It showed a provocative young woman in brassière and panties. She wears a kid's ragamuffin cap on the back of her head and carries a slingshot. Two voyeur gendarmes are spying on her from over the top of a fence.

"Kid," the ad says, "de Lady de Paris. *Très 1968, très, très jeune, très, très, très feminin ... C'est Kid, le nouvel ensemble de Lady. Le soutien-gorge: 31 F. Le panty: 39.90 F. En blanc, marine et azur."*

This advertisement documented to my satisfaction that the soutien-gorge indeed does not support the throat. It also indicated, however, that the French do have the right word for panty.

But it seems to me that fifty million Frenchmen could have thought up a better word for *brassière* than *soutien-gorge.*

THE THANK-YOU NOTE

*Even Dylan Thomas
botched the job.*

Ever since the women's liberation movement first made contact with my consciousness, my wife and I have lived harmoniously according to a new and enlightened division of domestic chores; so I am surprised to find out that this arrangement has not been perfect in every particular.

I have only just learned that she is not entirely satisfied that it should be her responsibility to write thank-you notes after we have been pleasantly entertained at someone's house, as well as the other kinds of written communications that occasionally are required, even in this day of the telephone.

I had noticed, certainly, that she often fell behind in her correspondence, sometimes months behind; but I ascribed this to her habit of putting things off, not to any frivolous notion that writing thank-you notes was my job, not hers.

What brought it out was my comment on one of the questions asked by Anne Wittels in her little book *I Wonder: A Satirical Study of Sexist Semantics*. Ms. Wittels wrote as follows: "They both have parents, grandparents, aunts, uncles, cousins, etc. How come she's the one who sends all the thank-you letters and birthday cards?"

To which I countered as follows: "Well, if they both have a fireplace, how come he's the one who chops the wood?" I thought it was an answer that deserved nothing less, even from Ms. Wittels, than a sincere "Touché." My surprise may be imagined, then, when my wife said, "Well, why *should* the wife have to write the thank-you letters?"

The question implied such heresy that I hardly knew how to answer it. One might as well ask why the wife should have to bear the children. I can think of no other domestic necessity that more clearly belongs in the wife's list of responsibilities, if indeed it can be thought of as a responsibility at all. I myself think of writing thank-you notes as more of a special treat.

It is a tradition that I can hardly imagine a woman wishing to challenge. The irony of it is that writing thank-you notes was a privilege gained by women in one of their earlier liberation movements. Until the beginning of the last century, the art of writing social notes was almost exclusively practiced by men. In the world of Samuel Johnson, James Boswell and Sydney Smith, for example, the intellectual community of London was held together by the terse and graceful messages that were passed promptly between such gentlemen by the more efficient postal service of that day.

If women wrote notes at all, it was more likely to be in the service of some infidelity or intrigue. The romantic fiction of that period is amply furnished with such missives, and the plot often turns on their untimely discovery. Such indiscretions were available only to the women of the upper classes, however, their common sisters being unschooled in the literary graces.

Thus in the nineteenth century when young women who had taken lessons in reading and writing became housewives or spinsters, there being no other respectable vocations, they felt a need to exercise these precious skills. They were of course not encouraged to write poetry or novels, despite the success of an occasional Elizabeth Barrett or George Eliot, so most women turned their creative talents and literary skills to the composition of thank-you letters. I imagine that, if the tens of thousands of thank-you letters that must have been written by English ladies in the nineteenth century could be retrieved from trunks and attics and published, with judicious editing, they would constitute a treasure of detail, insight and comment on the manners, morals and personalities of one of history's most vigorous and successful nations at the moment of its greatest glory.

That women of today should surrender this hard-won field to their mates is the kind of folly that the women's movement promotes with its peculiar notion that husbands and wives should share *every* kind of domestic responsibility.

The fact is that if women did not write thank-you notes they would never get written, because most husbands cannot write the most elementary letter. Once they have turned in their final college essay, under duress, they sink into semi-illiteracy, which serves them well enough in most of the enterprises their wives are so eager to get into.

If husbands wrote the thank-you notes they would read something like this:

Dear Fred:
Hey, great party, man. Thanks a bunch. Like I say, you can't beat the grub and the hooch at the Whipples. Hey, where you been hiding that niece of yours? Wow-EE! Oh, Kathy says say thanks to the Mrs.

Yours, Bill

If women stop writing thank-you notes, as I have told my wife over and over, polite society will tear apart like an old paper antimacassar, and civilization will not last long after that.

My position on this question is sustained, I believe, by the several graceful thank-you notes I have received from women for pointing it out.

On the other hand, some women seem reluctant to accept the responsibility or privilege of writing thank-you notes, and some even question my finding that most husbands are incapable of writing a literate and gracious thank-you note.

"The very idea that we women should actually be grateful for the privilege granted us, upon marriage, of being allowed to express in writing another individual's feelings of gratitude, sympathy, etc., is incredible and ridiculous," writes Margaret Lindstrom.

"Just as a small sample of refuting the argument

that the male is 'incapable' of letter-writing," she goes on, "allow me to quote Dylan Thoma (a Welsh-man like yourself) from one of many letters of thanks or apology he wrote [this one to Lawrence Durrell].

Dear Lawrence,
I forgot to thank you for the pound, crisper than celery and sweeter than sugar oh the lovely sound, not through ingratitude, it's as welcome as a woman is cleft, but through work (half a poem about energy), sloth (in a chair looking at my feet or the mirror or unread novels or count-ing patterns on the floor to see if I can work out a system for my football pools or watching my wife knit or dance), depression (because, mostly, there weren't more pounds from more people), small habits (from bar-billiards to broadcast talks, slick-bonnetted Hampshire roadhouses and socialist teas), love unqualified, the near-ness of Bournemouth, colds and pains in the head and your *Black Book* about which more in another and longer letter....

"Now," says Mrs. Lindstrom, "isn't that eloquent and descriptive? Lest you argue that Dylan Thomas is a rare exception and wrote because he loved to write anyway, I would like to add that I worked for five years for a man who never failed to write thoughtful notes and letters of sympathy, gratitude, congratula-tions, etc. He was a very busy man, too, serving as the consul general of Sweden and as a very busy attorney, but that did not seem to stop him from being civil-ized."

Yes, I was about to observe that Dylan Thomas was rather a rare exception, and this objection is not to be offset by Mrs. Lindstrom's backup example of a consul general, among whose duties as a diplomat would surely be the writing of thank-you and congratulatory letters. (My guess is that Mrs. Lindstrom knows about those letters only because she had to type them and put them into English.)

As for the Thomas letter Mrs. Lindstrom offers into evidence, one can hardly imagine a letter more alien to the kind I had in mind—the simple, polite, unpretentious note written by a wife in behalf of her husband and herself, thanking a hostess for a pleasant weekend or evening, or for any other act of civility and friendship.

In the first place, Dylan is not writing to his hostess, who presumably had gone to some trouble to appease his notorious appetites, but to another poet, and only to thank him for the loan of a pound. Thomas was always short of money, and obviously used a social invitation as a chance to make a touch.

Notice that, except for the money, Thomas doesn't thank Durrell or Mrs. Durrell for anything. He contents himself with his bibulous introspections, including a gratuitously sexist remark about women, a whine about money, and a passing mention of Durrell's book, which obviously he hasn't opened yet.

That the letter is shamefully tardy may be deduced from the several diversions that have kept him from the writing of it. Thomas has written half a poem, mooned about the house looking at his feet and so on, watched his wife knit and dance and probably mend his socks, played games, visited road-houses, gone to teas, made love (unqualified), and done whatever it was he did at nearby Bournemouth.

Mrs. Lindstrom finds his letter eloquent and descriptive. It would be vain of me to deny the powers of a poet as gifted as Dylan Thomas, but I am not persuaded that he should have assumed the writing of domestic thank-you notes. Though she could not have had much time for it, with three children and her knitting and mending and a self-indulgent poet to care for, I have an idea that Mrs. Thomas would have written a better one, perhaps like this:

Dear Mrs. Durrell;
Thank you for the lovely holiday. The mutton joint was delicious. Also thank your hubby for the quid. Dylan would have written to thank him but he has been very busy looking at his feet and half-writing a poem and all.

Sincerely yours,
Caitlin Thomas

Yes, I believe it's a woman's job.

POETS OF THE LOCKER ROOM

Should he of stood in bed?

Our language is not made by professors of English at Harvard, or graduate linguistics students at California State Long Beach, or by the editors of the *Atlantic* and other literary oracles. It is made largely by unschooled people who are trying to express their thoughts. Language gets its impulse from the genius that resides in the human species; after that it simply follows the line of least resistance.

If you want to keep up with trends in the language, you have to read the sports pages, as well as the literary and scientific journals. At least that is true when jocks are quoted accurately (excepting a few blips), and not misquoted by sports writers who think they understand the subjunctive mood and put it into the mouths of defensive tackles who have never been in the subjunctive mood in their lives.

More often we find quarterbacks quoted as having used a subjunctive, evidently because of the notion, widespread among sports writers, that quarterbacks are smarter than other people, especially other jocks. Thus, we read that a quarterback has said, "I sensed that if I were to win, I would have to pass more."

That quarterback not only used the Douglas Mac-Arthur first person singular as a pronoun for his entire team, but also used the subjunctive *were* where it was not required.

On the other hand, in the moment of victory or defeat, athletes often come up with spontaneous locutions of ingenuity and force.

Some years ago a prizefighter named Leon Spinks, then recognized by some authorities as heavyweight champion of the world (having won a decision over Muhammad Ali), was accused of being stimulated in that fight by a drug taken from "a little black bottle" concealed in his hand. Spink's comment was set forth in a headline as follows:

SPINKS: "I AIN'T DENYING THERE WASN'T NO BOTTLE"

You could wait a long time for a triple negative that makes perfect sense, and I hope it is not thought that I am making fun of Spinks. I cherish his remark as an example of the vigor and adaptability of the language. He had something to say, and he got it said.

In dealing with the serious accusation against him, Spinks did not say there was no bottle. Neither did he say there was one. What he said was that the bottle contained water, not a drug—if there was a bottle, and he wasn't saying there wasn't.

Pedants who insist on logic in language might have a hard time with "I ain't denying there wasn't no bottle." I have tried to parse it, to see where it comes out, but it has too many turns. Actually, if the word *denying* is taken as a negative, it is a quadruple negative, not simply a triple, and a quadruple negative is beyond the powers of even the most devious British playwright. Playwrights use the language. People like Spinks invent it.

Another of the most graphic statements of the twentieth century is the remark made in the late 1940s by a heavyweight champion's manager after his lost a fight: "We should have stood in bed."

What he meant, of course, was that considering the way things turned out, he and his fighter would have been better off if they had not got out of bed that morning. It is interesting to note that he used the managerial *we*, rather than the MacArthurian *I*.

The meaning of his remark was so starkly clear that its grammar was unimportant. All of us who read that quotation realized that he had expressed our own feelings in a way we had never quite been able to do. All of us have had days in which we should have stood in bed, and in fact the phrase was so welcome that it has become a cliché.

Ironically, a certain type of solecism that has become endemic to the sports world may be blamed indirectly on Edwin Newman and his best-sellers about the abuse of the language, especially by sports reporters and announcers. Unnerved by Newman's reprimands, television sports announcers who have no firm grasp of the differences between *he* and *him*, or *I* and *me*, are going to *I* and *he*, when it should be, according to grammar, *me* and *him*. So we hear such things as, "There's nobody between he and the goal line."

What has happened is that the announcers, having read Newman (and William Safire and John Simon too, presumably), and not wanting to be caught using bad grammar in front of sixty million people, say *I* and *he* because they have some vague recollection from their schooldays that *me* and *him* aren't nice, and the subjective forms of the pronoun somehow sound more elegant.

I am not in a good position to quarrel with this tendency, since I happen to make my faults in the opposite court. I am much more likely to say "It's me" than "It's I," and so on with *him, them* and *us.* My defense is that I use *me, him* and *them* in such cases because it's the vernacular; the way we talk. On the other hand, the use of *I* and *he* for *me* and *him* is a pretentious error, since one is avoiding the vernacular, the familiar, for the sake of an imaginary elegance.

Even so, the practice is now so pervasive that *he* and *I* are replacing *me* and *him*, and people like me, who write notes thanking someone for having my wife and me to dinner, will soon have to say my wife and I or be thought illiterate. Alas, people who might be heard by half the adults in the nation on a particular Sunday have a lot more influence on the way we talk than Newman has.

If only those sports announcers didn't take themselves so seriously they would use the language of the playing field and the locker room, and it would be good English.

Speaking of errors, I am obliged to recall a paragraph for reexamination. It was the one in which I quoted a heavyweight champion's manager as saying, "We should have stood in bed."

Not only did I attribute that remark to the wrong author and the wrong decade, according to Frances G. Sweeney and one or two other vigilant readers, but I also misquoted it.

"Let me be among the first of the petty faultfinders," writes Miss Sweeney, "who will jump on you for the quotation, 'We should have stood in bed.' The incorrect auxiliary 'have' stands out like a sore thumb. In the case of a phrase such as 'stood in bed,' it should be obvious that the correct auxiliary is *of*.

"With this in mind," she continues, "I went to my Bartlett's and, looking under *stood*, quickly found the quotation, 'I should of stood in bed.' It is attributed to Joe Jacobs (1896-1940) who, according to Bartlett's, 'left a sickbed to go to Detroit in October, 1935, to attend the World's Series. He bet on Chicago which lost to Detroit. When he returned to New York he made this comment to the sports writers who came to interview him.'

"I am sorry that this destroys your point about the managerial *we*, but at least Jacobs was a heavyweight champion's manager, as you said."

Meaning no disrespect for Bartlett's, I must question its rendering of *World Series* as *World's Series*. This is simply not American English, and nothing is more American than the World Series. In fact, I would be willing to bet that Joe Jacobs called it the World *Serious*, like the characters in Ring Lardner's immortal baseball stories.

As to the other facts, though, no doubt Bartlett's is right. But I remember vividly that a fight manager or promoter (perhaps Mike Jacobs) made that remark after a disastrous spectacle, and my colleagues and I at the *Daily News* were much exhilarated by it. He must have stolen it from Joe.

Anyway, I count it a much more grievous error on my part to have mangled the quotation by substituting the auxiliary verb *have* for *of*. That was simply illiterate of me.

In checking my Bartlett's, I found that it was also Joe Jacobs who first said, "We was robbed!" The circumstances as described in Bartlett's: "After the fight between Max Schmeling and Jack Sharkey, June 21, 1932, when Sharkey had been awarded the decision and the heavyweight title, Jacobs, Schmeling's manager, shouted into the radio microphone this protest which was heard from coast to coast."

I hate to admit an error wtihout making some capital out of it, and I'm happy that correcting this one gives me a chance to acknowledge some other quotations which, if they are not in Bartlett's, certainly ought to be.

One comes from Lupe Hinckle and is attributed to the immortal Casey Stengel: "A lot of people my age are dead at the present time."

The other, from Richard Hemphill, is attributed to one of Casey's pupils, Yogi Berra: "If the fans won't come out to the stadium to watch the game, we can't stop 'em." (This is reminiscent of Samuel Goldwyn's comment on some movie, perhaps one of his own: "Don't miss it if you can.")

By the way, Leon Spinks's triple negative reminded Eric Elfman of something his father said to him during an argument in which Eric had just made what he considered a winning point: "I can't possibly fail to disagree with you less."

"This brought me up short," Elfman says, "and it took me about a week to figure out that it meant 'I agree with you.'"

All this may be of little concern to most people, but I could care less.

I hoped we were finished with Joe Jacobs and could let him return to Bartlett's and his rest, but evidently immortality is not that easily won.

I am reminded that a question remains: Did Jacobs say "I should *have* stood in bed," or "I should *of* stood in bed," or "I *should've* stood in bed," or "I *shoulda* stood in bed."?

It may be thought that we are giving this question more attention than it's worth, but I remind the reader that Jacobs's words are preserved in Bartlett's along with the best of Milton, Kipling and Susan B. Anthony, among others, and ought not to be enshrined in mangled form.

Now I am assailed by those who insist that what sounds like *of* is simply the contraction of *should have*, that is, *should've*, and by yet others who insist that it was neither *should of* nor *should've*, but *shoulda*.

"We all use *should've*—a contraction of *should have*," writes George I. Foster. "Try to pronounce '*should've*' without making it sound like *should of*. Writers write *should of* in an effort to be funny."

On the other hand, Alan Keogh writes: "In regard to the controversy over *should have*, as against *should of*, any English language purist could inform you that correct usage here should be, *I shoulda stood in bed.*"

By chance the Jacobs quote was aired again by Jim Murray in his column. "In the World Series of 1935," he recalled, "which was played in biting cold between the Detroit Tigers and Chicago Cubs, Joe Jacobs, the fight manager, later famous for giving the Nazi salute in Germany with his hat on, cigar in his mouth, and his fingers crossed behind his back, left a sickbed to attend the games, surveyed the overcoated scene with his false teeth chattering, and pronounced, 'I shoulda stood in bed.'"

I hope Murray's version (except for the *shoulda*) reaches the editors of Bartlett's, because it is much more vivid than theirs, and worthier of the subject. But I now have in hand what I consider an authoritative eyewitness account of the birth of the Jacobs classic, and while Murray's paragraph deserves immortality, it seems beyond doubt that he has the grammar wrong. Thanks to Bob Hunter, who saves clippings in a shoe box, I have a column about Jacobs by John Lardner, from *Newsweek*, January 18, 1960. In it Lardner noted that he found the Bartlett's entry erroneous, and had written to correct it.

"Why quibble, you ask?" wrote Lardner. "Well, friends, a man has got to quibble in defense of the facts of the only Familiar Quotation that was ever coined in his presence."

He thereupon described the circumstances at some length, concluding as follows: "It was the first game of the Series (1935, in Detroit) and the coldest day of sport that I can remember. The wind knifing through the press box—where Joe sat in the row behind me—

flayed one's skin and bruised one's knee bones. Strong men without flasks were dying. In the third or fourth inning, I can't pretend to remember which, Joe Jacobs arose and pointed his nose toward his hotel. 'I should of stood in bed,' he said to all within earshot.''

I am convinced that what Jacobs said was *should of*. For one thing, Lardner heard him. For another, my guess is that Jacobs thought *should of* was good grammar. I'm sure that *should of* is exactly what he would have written, had he put it down on paper. *Should of* may sound to the careless ear like *should've*, but John Lardner, like his father, the incomparable Ring, did not have a careless ear.

I have done my duty. History and language are served. And as I say, I could care less. That doesn't mean, as some readers seem to think, that I couldn't care less. Careless people, when they say "I could care less," mean they don't care. When I say "I could care less," I mean I care. Because I do.

PERSON OVERBOARD

Goodbye to the telephone lineman.

One of the lesser heroes of American legend is the telephone lineman, and he too seems in danger of vanishing from the scene, in name at least—one more victim of the notion that woman's lot will be improved if all words ending in "man" are expunged from the language.

Though never given the kind of worship we devote to our athletes, singers and outlaws, the telephone lineman has enjoyed our respect and admiration. He was a rakish figure in his work clothes. With those spiked boots for climbing telephone poles and the tools of his trade hanging from his belt, he was reminiscent of the gunfighter, another legendary figure with whom he shared the winning of the West.

The lineman's work was risky and spectacular. We hardly envied him on wintry days, when the dark sky was crackling with electricity and he had to shinny up a pole to repair a break so the neighborhood could have its telephone service. There was no margin for error up there among the high-tension wires, and now and then something would go wrong and a man would be killed in his harness.

I remember from my boyhood an inspiring book called *Slim the Telephone Lineman,* or something like that. And of course more recently country singer Glen Campbell immortalized the breed with "The Wichita Lineman."

But now, I am told by a news release from the General Telephone Company of California, the word "lineman" has been dropped from its list of job titles "in response to a recommendation from the Fair Employment Practices Commission."

From now on, a telephone lineman will be known as a "plant construction installer." So a neat, simple, graphic term—lineman—is buried, and the American language slips a bit further into the morass of gobbledygook.

It is not only the word *lineman* that has been eliminated in General Telephone's desexification program. Another honorable occupation—draftsman—will henceforth be known as "drafting plans drawer." As in the case of *lineman,* we now have three words where previously one served very well.

The company has gone all the way down the list, changing its "man" words to other words, usually two or three other words, A pressman is now a printing press operator, a repairman is a plant maintainer, and a warehouseman is a warehouse attendant.

I hope no one thinks I disapprove of women working as telephone linemen or in any other of these jobs which traditionally may have been held by men. I imagine a healthy young woman can climb a telephone pole as easily as a man, and would probably be even more fascinating to watch.

But why can't a woman telephone lineman be called a lineman? It was an earlier generation's attempt to feminize occupational titles that gave us such monstrous words as authoress, aviatrix and even, God help us, doctoress. Today, happily, women may be called authors, aviators and doctors, and no one thinks of these words as sexist or masculine.

Lineman would quickly become common and accepted. No one would think of the word as containing the word "man," anymore than women think of the word *woman* itself as containing the word *man*. If they are looking for sexist words to eliminate, *woman* (the word *man* once meant person) should have been the first to go.

Such words as policewoman and congresswoman are in wide use, however, though we don't need them. Policeman and congressman would serve both sexes. But I will agree to almost any compromise to avoid that ridiculous suffix "person." Happily, "person" will probably fail in the long run because no one who has the slightest respect for the language can bear the sound of it, especially when it turns up at the end of a good old word that has been brutally cut short to have it grafted on.

The other day a reader sent me a copy of the student newspaper of the University of California at Santa Cruz in which first-year students are referred to as "freshpersons." Is that what the freedom of speech movement has brought us to? *Freshpersons* is a word so awkward and bleak that it shows us just how silly we've become.

One of the things I liked best about my brief life at college was girl freshmen. I hope they're here to stay.

And someday I hope there will be an inspiring book for little girls called *Sue, the Telephone Lineman.* That is the way the language will truly be desexed.

Meanwhile it is heartening that the U.S. Naval Academy at Annapolis has resisted pressure to call its women students midshippersons, and will call them women midshipmen.

It is good news, but it would have been better if the Navy hadn't chosen to put that *women* in front of *midshipmen.* I suspect, in fact, that the Associated Press was in error, and that women enrolled as undergraduates at the academy will be referred to simply as midshipmen, as they should be.

In deciding to call them midshipmen the Navy has merely come round to the reasonable view that midshipman is a rank, and that it may be applied to a person of either sex, just as a foreman, whether male or female, is a person in charge of a jury, and a chairman is a person in charge of a committee.

Back in World War I when the U.S. Marine Corps formed the Women's Reserve, women enlistees were called "women reserves." But that had a rather evangelical ring to it. It might have been the name of a Baptist choir, which would not do. So in World War II they dropped the *reserves* and called them "women marines." Then even that began to seem silly. If they were marines, wasn't that good enough? Were the men called "men marines?"

To the everlasting credit of the Corps, its women

now are called marines, and for all I know they are also entitled to that honored nickname Leathernecks. I don't keep up with the Army and Navy, but I believe they now call their women soldiers and sailors.

The notion that a woman oughtn't to be called soldier or sailor has no more merit than the notion that a women oughtn't to be called marine, carpenter or journeyman. There used to be a surefire line in the movies where Ava Gardner or Carole Lombard fought off the restless natives and stayed up through the steamy night nursing a fevered Clark Gable or Robert Taylor. When the fellow finally came out of his delirium and saw her standing there, worried half-crazy and about to fall in her tracks from exhaustion, he would look up into her hollow eyes and whisper, "Good soldier," and the tears would come and she would sink to his wasted chest and you knew the crisis was over. I must have heard it a hundred times, and the fellow never said "woman soldier."

Another exciting development is the decision by the Los Angeles Board of Education to let girls play with boys on interscholastic teams in baseball, basketball and soccer. Linguists need have no fear of any remodeling of the names of the various positions in basketball, unless some girl resents being called forward; nor will sexually integrated soccer result in any awkward juggling of suffixes.

There could be trouble in baseball, though, and I think the Board of Education would be well advised to ensure at once, by fiat, that a third baseman is not to be called a girl third baseman, or third basewoman or third baseperson, but simply third baseman, which is the name that goes with the position. And God help her when she has to come in on the squeeze or sacrifice.

It is said the board is also thinking about allowing girls to play with boys in football, wrestling and water polo. Again, I see no problems except in football, where some sexist coach or sportswriter may want to call a female guard or tackle a linewoman or lineperson or perhaps girl lineman or girl of the line. Again, it's something the board should be able to control.

Wrestling between boys and girls should create no problems at all, that I can see. It is of course a one-on-one sport, and we can simply call boys *he* and girls *she*.

Whatever happens, the prospects are exciting indeed, and I only wish, as I do about so many of the changes that have come in these liberated times, that they had come a few years sooner.

There was a girl named Lucille (freckles, sandy hair) who used to beat me regularly in the 75-yard dash. She never knew it, because of course it was unthought of in those days, but what I really wanted to do with her was wrestle.

Boy, what a good soldier I'll bet she turned out to be.

Though the absurd word chairperson and all other person-words will in good time die of their own absurdity, such forms continue to be coined as if the invention of person-words were a crazy parlor game, like the "knock-knock" jokes of the 1950s. (For example: cowperson, caveperson, and Portuguese-person-of-war).

But they aren't all meant as jokes, even the funniest ones. Some time ago the city of Del Mar, a place of salubrious climate on the Pacific Coast near San Diego, officially adopted the phrase *sewer access structures* in the place of *manholes*. This tongue-twister was introduced by Hervey Sweetwood, a young management consultant and city councilman, during his term as mayor.

There seem to be two reasons why the campaign against the suffix or prefix *man* enjoys such a vogue in the bureaucracy. First, legislators are happy to give pressure groups what they want if it's something that doesn't cost any money, like changing the word manhole to either personhole or sewer access structure. Also, as a reading of almost any government letter, statement, decree or memorandum will show, the bureaucracy loves gobbledygook, and is happy to take in any word or phrase that is inflated, pretentious or unintelligible.

I suppose I ought to say again that I am with my fellow feminists in wishing to open up more jobs to women. That young Sweetwood in Del Mar meant to open up sewer work to women is commendable, and in the spirit of our times. But I think he could have accomplished this without changing manholes to sewer access structures. If a girl wants to work in a sewer she will not be discouraged by the fact that the word manhole has a man in it.

The term sewer access structure bothers me not only because it is wordy and pretentious, but because it is also inexact, at least to one who is not an engineer. Perhaps in a technical sense a hole is a structure; but to most of us a structure is something of substance, like a doghouse or a bridge, and a hole is a hole.

By the way, I don't know what Del Mar calls manhole covers, but it seems unlikely that they would simply call them sewer access structure covers. My guess is that they are called sewer access structure closure devices.

I was hoping that the attempt to make sewer work more attractive to women by unsexing the word manhole would have died of its own absurdity, until I heard from Sweetwood himself.

"Your defense of manhole," he wrote, "confuses me, for I believe this word must have entered the English language from popular slang usage, a source— you often point out—that corrupts the language. So perhaps it is time to rectify this historic mistake and coin a new word which has a more precise meaning.

"Manhole," he continued, "reflects the value of the era in which it was coined. In those days the only people allowed to work in sewers were men and hence an entryway to a sewer was logically called a manhole. In fact the Random House dictionary defines manhole as 'a hole, usually with a cover, through which a *man* may enter a sewer, drain, steam boiler, etc.' (emphasis added). The linguistic reminders of sexual discrimination should be removed from the language as their original intent becomes inaccurate.

"Now I admit," he added, "that sewer access structure may be a bit of a tongue twister, but at least it has advanced the debate and perhaps may lead to a better solution."

Sweetwood was in error when he said I had often

pointed out that slang corrupts the language. Most slang words have their vogue and pass away, but many stay because they are vivid, graphic and needed. If all the words that had entered English as slang were suddenly forgotten we would all be talking gobbledygook.

As for Sweetwood's idea that only men were allowed to work in sewers in the era in which the word manhole was coined, it is enlightening to note that the *Oxford English Dictionary* traces the word to 1793, and cites this use of it in 1841: "to make apertures or man-holes . . . to enable *persons* . . . to enter and cleanse the sewers" (emphasis added).

So it seems to have been understood at least 188 years ago that sewer work was open to persons, as well as men. I suspect that if women didn't get into sewers it was probably because they didn't want to, not because manhole had a man in it.

Del Mar's contribution to the decline of simple English in government might be taken as merely a local diversion, except that young Sweetwood evidently had an evangelical urge to spread his gospel to other little towns with a manhole problem.

When Sweetwood found out that the mayor and city council of Woonsocket, R.I., had encountered heavy opposition for changing manholes in Woonsocket to personholes, he wrote the Woonsocket mayor, according to a story in the *San Diego Union*, advising him "to stick with the fight against linguistic sexism and try 'sewer access structures.'"

The following story from the *Cranston* (R.I.) *Journal-Bulletin* describing the Woonsocket City Council's final action gives us the happy ending.

WOONSOCKET DROPS THE HOLE THING

WOONSOCKET—Don't worry about walking across the street and falling into an open 'person-hole' any more. They no longer exist. Person-holes were abolished by an embarrassed City Council last night. Councilmen decided that the street manholes that other cities have been using for years were good enough for them, too.

The story goes on to say that the vote was unanimous, and "onlookers laughed and applauded."

I have a feeling that this may have been the turning point, and that in time Woonsocket will come to mean the end of the person-plague, as Waterloo means the end of Napoleon and Watergate the end of Nixon.

WHAT DO YOU CALL
A LIVE-IN LOVER?

*All the world
loves an..uh...um...er....*

Since marriage-like relationships without benefit of city hall or clergy are now so commonplace as hardly to raise an eyebrow, I am not surprised at the widespread interest in what the parties to such arrangements can be called.

Within a few days of each other a physician and a mother-in-law have asked me what we should call unmarried couples, since they are not legally husband and wife; and, even more important, what they should call each other's mother, father, sister, brother and so on.

In other words, is an unmarried young woman's lover her mother's son-in-law?

It was exactly that situation that prompted the mother-in-law to write. Obviously, she is not really the mother-in-law, but I am calling her that for lack of a better term, which shows how serious the problem is.

She does not look with unreconcilable disfavor on

her daughter's roommate or their intimate relationship; she simply wants to know what to call the chap, and herself. She thinks of him as a son-in-law, yet the very term "in-law" is contrary to the fact, and might be taken as an ironic barb.

This innocent woman's quandary is expressed in more scholarly language by Dr. Josephus Reynolds, who writes as follows:

"I have been asked by a friend whose daughter has been living openly with a young man out of wedlock whether there exists in the English language a word that would be suitable to designate either party to what we now recognize as a commonplace arrangement, and if not, whether I would accept the commission to create such an appellation...."

Dr. Reynolds began by eliminating the unsatisfactory words now in use. "Obviously," he says, "such terms as girlfriend and boyfriend would be inappropriate as their application does not exclude platonic relationships. Fiancée or fiancé would be totally misleading as they include the justifiable anticipation of a foreseeable eventuality....

"Thinking in a functional framework, I concluded that a single word embodying the attributes of love and friendship would convey the precise meaning applicable to the situation. In Latin *amor* means love, and *amicus*, friend, so the portmanteau, *amoricus* and *amorica*, appear to be eminently suitable designations that parents and others might employ in referring to those liberated individuals who hitherto had not enjoyed the dignity of a specific denomination."

I think Dr. Reynolds has labored nobly at his commission, but I doubt that *amoricus* and *amorica* will catch on. While his suggestion may be etymologically sound, even brilliant, it seems to me to lack popular appeal. We are talking about earthy relationships here. Mother, father, son, daughter, husband, wife—these are all earthy words from Old English, and I just don't think a Latin word can make it. Imagine a young woman bursting into a room full of gimlet-eyed aunts and uncles and announcing, "Hello, everyone, I'd like you to meet Freddie, my amoricus!"

Even if we can imagine our roomies referring to each other as amoricus and amorica, where does this leave the poor mothers, assuming they approve of the liaison and want to be included in introductions. After all, the amorica's amoricus isn't her mother's amoricus, so she couldn't call him her amoricus, or even her amoricus-in-law, since in-law is out.

I suppose she could call him her son-in-love-and-friendship, which Dr. Reynolds could render into Latin if he liked. Come to think of it, son-in-love-and-friendship isn't bad. With wide use, it would quickly be shortened to son-in-love, which would not only be accurate but euphonious, and if spoken with a slight slur, or after a martini or two, could easily pass for son-in-law.

Taking it one step further, why not shorten *amoricus* and *amorica* by cutting them down to simple *amor?* Translate it back to English and what do you have? Love. Now we hear our young woman saying, "Hello, everyone, I'd like you to meet my love."

It's not as casual as *chum*, which doesn't say enough. It's not as earthy as *mate*, which says too much. It's not as erotic as *lover*, which is too candid.

Love, noun; a person with whom another lives in conjugal harmony without benefit of clergy.

By George, that may be it. How happy that woman who wrote me will be when her daughter's amoricus first calls her his mother-in-love!"

To my surprise, many of the letters I have received in response to this amiable proposal are humorless denunciations of cohabiting sons and daughters as *sinners*. For many persons, some of them obviously parents who themselves are victims of this troublesome language deficiency, the only words we need can be found in the Bible: *adulteress* and *fornicator*. I had no idea so many of us were in a position to cast first stones.

On the other hand, there are some who agree with me that the lack of a good word for the parties to this very popular kind of relationship is causing us more embarrassment than the relationship itself. We should really be disappointed that a language as virile as ours has produced nothing much better than such hoary terms as *companionate marriage* and *free love*, both of which have a slight odor of Bertrand Russell and Havelock Ellis.

That the problem is not limited to the young and their families is shown by a woman who writes from Arcadia: "I am fifty-six years old and 'dating' or 'going with' a man who is sixty-two. It's silly to refer to him as my 'boyfriend,' and my 'friend' isn't quite enough. 'The man I am going with' is an awkward expression. Since we are not living together, 'my love' wouldn't fit, and 'my lover' is a little too much, especially since I have teenagers at home. We are not engaged, so 'fiancé' isn't correct. Also, even for young people, I have always disliked the expression 'going steady,' but what would you call a relationship that is more than a friendship but not an engagement?"

Can those who like the words *adulteress* and *fornicator* help this poor woman?

I am happy to learn from Dr. Barry Singer of the California State University Long Beach psychology department that the problem has not escaped academic notice. Singer co-edits the social science journal *Alternative Lifestyles,* and recently wrote a piece for it called "Mom, This Is My Umm. . . ."

On the day he completed that article, Singer recalls, an almost identical article with an almost identical title appeared in *The Times* ("Hello, I'd Like You to Meet My . . . er") by Robert Toth. Despite this unsettling coincidence, Singer published, pointing out that "the appearance of *The Times* article is perhaps a testimonial to the timeliness and importance of our semantic effort."

Curiously, I have also received a letter from an Alhambra reader, Marjorie Gagne, in which she says, "Thought you might get a kick out of what our family uses—'Meet my son and his . . . um . . . er. . . .'"

This suggests that some such term as *um, um-er,* or *ummer* may ultimately find its way into the language, and all our deliberate attempts to coin a word will have been just mental calisthenics.

Meanwhile, it may be that the elusive word has all the time been in our possession, delivered to us inadvertently by the most unlikely source—the bureaucracy itself.

I mean the word *posslq,* an acronym for Persons of Opposite Sex Sharing Living Quarters, a phrase found in the 1980 U.S. Census form.

Posslq (which I assume should be pronounced *poss'l-cue,* or perhaps *pozz'l-cue*) was first called to my attention by Dr. Albert A. Kattus of Inglewood, a cardiologist, who happened to hear Charles Osgood use it on "Newsbreak," CBS Radio, in one of his charming radio essays.

Dr. Kattus was so excited by *posslq* that he wrote to Osgood, who graciously sent him a transcript of his talk, in which he gave credit to William Rukeyser of *Money* magazine for discovering the status identification from which the acronym and the word are derived.

"The very word we've been looking for!" Osgood exclaimed. "You can say, without so much as a blush, 'This is Deedee, my posslq.' Or 'Say hello to Franklin. We're posslqs.'"

To show that the word is adaptable to the highest form of literary art, Osgood went on to improve the great love lyric by Christopher Marlowe, which begins, "Come live with me and be my love," by interpolating this lovely couplet—

> *You live with me, and I with you*
> *And you will be my posslq.*

Nitpickers will see at once that Persons of Opposite Sex Sharing Living Quarters may be married persons; but that was not the intent of the phrase in the census. And in practice, the words will be taken to mean unmarried persons only, since there is such a need for it.

Since my belated discovery of this excellent word I have heard from Willard R. Espy, the playful New York wordsmith and author of *An Almanac of Words at Play*, who notes that he reflects on the word in

Another Almanac of Words at Play. With a third *s*, Espey points out, *possslq* could serve "Persons of Same Sex Sharing Living Quarters, a different breed."

Yes, *possslqs* may be a different breed, but they too need a word, as argued by Ed Slabotsky of Los Angeles: "You straights have never lived in fear of felony prosecution," he writes, "just whether to blush or not on making family introductions. So I salute all us posslqs and possslqs and long may we cohabit! In fact, you and Mrs. Smith are poosslqs. Why skip the preposition?" (Espey also favors keeping the first *o*, liking "the appropriately smoochy sound" *poosslq*.)

I myself prefer to stay with the original *posslq*, despite its shortcomings. It could be lost among the variations, and I think there are already some signs that it is catching on; if so, it is worth saving.

Nancy Abrams of Woodland Hills has sent me a classified ad from the *Dallas Morning News*, under Homes and Real Estate for Sale, as follows: *1900 Serenade. Young Married's, Room-Mates, or POSSL-Q'S will love this adorable one-owner traditional; 3 bedrooms, master with sitting area! Large living-den with WBFP. Bright kitchen.*

I have quoted "Young Married's," "Room-Mates," and "POSSLQ'S" exactly as they appear in the ad. I do not understand Texan, so it would be inappropriate for me to point out that there should be no apostrophe in *marrieds*, that *roommates* is one word and should not be hyphenated, and that *posslq*, though indeed an acronym, should not be spelled out in capitals. It is time we decapitalized it if it is to survive and fill an urgent need in our vocabularies.

Nor would I be petty enough to point out that *posslqs,* being plural, does not take an apostrophe. It is fascinating to speculate, though, how important these trivial errors might be to strangers trying to decode our language. If *young married's* and *posslq's* are simply plurals they will wonder then what those apostrophes are doing in them. For surely one of the first things anyone from another planet would deduce from reading a newspaper would be the proper function of the apostrophe. Anyone stupid enough not to figure that out would be too stupid to get here. (I am assuming that if I can figure out that *WBFP* means *wood-burning fireplace,* our visitors should have no great difficulty with *posslq.*)

In any case, we may now assume that the custom of persons of opposite sex sharing living quarters, and the term *posslq* itself, have been accepted, even by conservatives, as legitimate in our times. After all, it is hard to imagine any more conservative American type than a Texas realtor.

The Dallas ad will also make it evident that conventional marriage was still tolerated in the late twentieth century, along with unconventional, and that young marrieds were welcome to live on the 1900 block of Serenade Street, as well as roommates and posslqs.

Our visitors will also find out that somewhere late in the twentieth century our apostrophes went astray.

THE BEAUTIFUL AND THE UGLY

Could Beethoven have written an Asphalt Sonata?

When the lexicographer Wilfred Funk died several years ago his obituary recalled that back in the 1920s he had compiled a list of what he considered the ten most beautiful words in the English languge, a list which, of course, stirred up a great deal of harmless controversy and brought forth any number of alternative lists.

Dr. Funk's list, which I first read as a schoolboy, was as follows: *dawn, hush, lullaby, murmuring, tranquil, mist, luminous, chimes, golden* and *melody*.

Recently the columnist Godfrey Smith of the *London Sunday Times* asked his readers to submit their lists of the ten most beautiful words, and offered a bottle of Bollinger champagne to the person whose list was the best. My knowledge of this affair is based solely on a subsequent column, and while it reviews the lists submitted, it does not say how Smith proposed to judge them and to whom the Bollinger was given.

What he did, however, was compile a "master list" of the ten words most often occurring in the various lists submitted. "It was like watching the fortunes of a general election as the votes poured in," he wrote, "and a race all week between *melody* and *velvet* for the top spot. Finally they tied."

There was also a tie for third place: *gossamer* and *crystal.* Then came *autumn, peace, tranquil, twilight* and *murmur;* and in a tie for tenth place, *mellifluous, whisper* and *caress.* Three runners-up were also bunched together: *silken, willow* and *mellow.* Others, more or less in order, were *lullaby, dawn, shimmer, silver, marigold, golden, dream, harmony, blossom, champagne, dusk, sleep, magic, love, mist, darling* and *laughter.*

I wonder whether we regard words as beautiful partly because of what they mean or simply because of their sound. Would *murmur,* for example, fall as softly on our ears if it meant belch? And would *belch* sound ugly, as it does, if it meant murmur?

I compiled a list of ten words I regarded as ugly: *belch, grub, slop, grouch, asphalt, snob, quack, headache, snake* and *crabgrass.* Would any of them sound beautiful if they meant, dawn, hush, lullaby, et cetera, instead of what they do? Would *asphalt* be lovely if it meant moonlight? Could Beethoven have written an Asphalt Sonata?

I doubt it. Does it mean that we tend to give ugly words to ugly thoughts?

As I said at the time of Dr. Funk's death: "Dr. Funk's list might appeal to romantic schoolgirls, brides and others who live in a misty gold ephemeral cocoon of illusion. But there are other beautiful words, too, with harder edges and a wilder kind of music. What about these? *Machine. Missile. Escalate.*

Fail-safe. Detonation. Fusion. Megaton. Mushroom. Holocaust. Oblivion. These are the beautiful words of our time.''

Oddly, those ten words don't seem to give me the chill they did when I first set them down, perhaps ten years ago. Is that because we are so used to them, and their implications, that they have lost their capacity to alarm and disturb us?

Are there other beautiful words that mean ugly things but which, when spoken, please the ear? Offhand, I think of *carcinoma* and *melanoma*. Truly lovely words in sound, but I can think of none more dreadful in the actuality.

Like Godfrey Smith of the *London Sunday Times*, I also turned to my readers, asking for their lists of ten words that sounded ugly to them but meant something beautiful, pleasant or good, and vice versa.

Perhaps the words beautiful and ugly are too demanding, and I should simply have said pleasant and unpleasant. *Kiss* is not, after all, an ugly word, but merely a rather unpleasant one; and a kiss, while often pleasant, is not invariably beautiful.

Having had no computer or accounting firm to help me tabulate the results, I made a crude attempt at determining which words were most frequently listed by going through the stacks of letters and reading the words aloud while my wife was making a tally on scratch pads. Its accuracy may have been affected not only by the instrinsic unreliability of this system but also by my simultaneously watching the Rams and 49ers on TV.

The beautiful but ugly words most often cited, somewhat in order of their popularity, are *malevo-*

lence, melancholy, felonious, urinal, malicious, phlegm, catastrophe, violence, euthanasia and *murder.* Actually, *gonorrhea, syphilis, venereal* and *catarrh* would have been in the top ten, but I left them out because I felt like it, and I am the judge. Medical terms are too easy.

Leading the tally of words that sound unpleasant but have a pleasant meaning are *pulchritude, pregnant, puce, osculate, orchid, peacock, music, crocus, purple* and *yogurt.* Among the runners-up are *luck, breast, kiss, liquor, sex* (and its variants), *girl, dog, cat, fudge, grackle, gazebo, gorgeous* and *gavotte.*

These are more interesting, it seems to me, than the beautiful sounding words. Some of them surprise me. I find *girl* a lovely word, also *gavotte, crocus* and *gazebo. Cat* certainly sounds unpleasant, but is a cat a pleasant object? Physically beautiful, yes; but they are also selfish, rapacious and wanton, and cat suits them very well. *Pregnant* is not a euphonious word, I agree; but whether the condition it names is pleasant or unpleasant is not for me to say. As for *grackle,* it is exactly suited to the voice and personality of that execrable bird.

Pat Voege of Glendale shows uncanny insight by guessing that I might not allow *cat* or *yogurt* as words that mean something pleasant. "If you don't think that either yogurt or cats are good, please substitute *turkey.*" I'm afraid I can't buy *turkey* either. A turkey is a turkey. But Miss Voege wins first prize (my compliments) for the ugly-beautiful word I least expected to find in a standard desk dictionary: *gutbucket,* which is an especially raucous kind of jazz.

Like others, Barbara Green of Monrovia found that the unpleasant words were hardest to think of. Those she came up with are *ganoid, habile, oxygen, panic, regnum, wallow, plucky, Terpsichore, eleemo-synary* and *punctual.* Miss Green must have a very sensitive ear. Except *ganoid,* and maybe *panic,* they all sound pleasant enough to me; and I would also diqualify *ganoid* because I don't happen to think ganoids in general are beautiful. (Ganoids, by the way, are not gonads.)

More interesting to me than the statistics are the tangential comments and digressions that this exercise brought forth. Illustrating the observation that words may seem either pleasant or unpleasant to us because of what they mean, Martha Avery of Newport Beach recalls: "The poet Edward Marsh, for many years secretary to Winston Churchill, asked a friend for his favorite English word. After some time the friend came up with *swallow.* '*Swallow?*' said Marsh. 'The noun or the verb?' (Sir Winston, I imagine, would have said, "The verb.")

Several readers, including Miss Avery, recall hearing that *cellar door* has been called the most beautiful word in the language. This judgment is ascribed variously to English professors, Frenchmen, and at least one Italian, the great Guglielmo Marconi himself.

Muriel Bradley recalls that when she was a little girl she named a much-loved Polynesian doll Pyorrhea. In this case ignorance was bliss. I doubt, though, that she spelled it right.

Roxana M. Dapper, among my correspondents, was alone in listing *men* as a word that sounds ugly but means something beautiful. On the other hand she listed *chauvinist* ("as in male chauvinist") among words that sound good but mean something bad. (Miss Dapper, by the way, shares first prize with another reader, Honey McCloud, for the most beguiling name among those responding to this challenge. First prize is my envy.)

Miss McCloud's list of pleasant-unpleasant words was among the better ones, in my judgment: *mildew, cruel, plaque, voodoo, mal de mer, decay, murder, tragic, malodorous* and *malign.* (I can't say that I like the sound of *plaque* or *tragic,* though.)

"Oh, for cry eye," wrote Lynden Keating in her inimitable style, "I had to put aside matters of pulsating significance—paying bills, flossing teeth, looking for blue birds, reading Ella Wheeler Wilcox, studying the Christian Science textbook, and sending hate mail to Jerry Falwell—to compile little compost heaps of words to you. . . ."

I quote from her letter to show that this was not a trivial exercise, since it could draw busy women like Miss Keating from such engagements. She was not the only one, either, who upended her priorities to get at this question: "I did not wish to become entangled in your word game," wrote Laurel Call Dugan of Cucamonga, a free-lance writer, "but it pursued me as I went about the house dusting and cleaning this morning. Now, as I sit at my typewriter trying to concentrate on an article I am writing, unrelated words keep breaking into my concentration. So, here goes.

"Bad things that sound pretty: *angel dust, cupidity, illicit, lascivious, latrine, nefarious, nemesis, venereal, wily, turbulent.* Good things that sound ugly: *cavort, crocus, crumpet, droll, gastronomy, influx, osculate, pew, phlox, Wiener schnitzel.*"

"I'll make you a side bet," wrote Kathy Thomas of San Pedro. "When the lists come in, those on the 'sound beautiful but mean ugly side' will be mostly polysyllabic (like tarantula). If a word is sufficiently mellifluous it can make even a spider sound good."

Mrs. Thomas was right. For example, the beautiful but bad list from Ira W. Holroyd of Chatsworth didn't have a one-syllable word in it: *abattoir, eviscerate, molest, larcenous, malicious, guillotine, napalm, malaise, lethal* and *macabre*. But there are four one-syllable words in his rather Freudian ugly but beautiful list, and only one with more than two syllables: *sexpot, yacht, picnic, leggy, pulchritude, ankle, buttock, bust, hug* and *grit*.

Lionel C. Meeker of Fallbrook puts *toad, diaper* and *egg* on his list of ugly words for beautiful things, pointing out that the egg, despite such metaphors as bad egg and egg on your face, is a beautiful object; that diaper once meant a diamond-patterned cloth; and that a toad is beautiful in the eyes of another toad.

My favorite list was this one: "Ugly sounding words for unugly things: *rance, praxis, scrod, fructify, suckle, spelunk, dunk, gravid, sapid, perspicacious* (and for good measure *nuzzle, nuptial and grass*). Pretty sounding words for not so pretty things: *larceny, gonorrhea, cadaver, melancholia, malign, felony, vandal, odious, contagious* and *knave*."

Those were Lynden Keating's. I don't like all of them. I don't even know what *rance* means. But what the heck, as Joe E. Brown said, "nobody's perfect."

Meanwhile, down in Australia, almost the same question was asked of his readers by Ian Warden, a columnist on *The Canberra Times*. I say almost the same, because Warden asked his readers merely to list words that were either beautiful or ugly, irrespective of their meanings. That made it a good deal easier.

It may not be proper for me to comment on Warden's lists, but I have chosen what I think are the ten most beautiful words from the winners, as follows: *parasol, larkspur, icicle, sparkle, cashmere, lapwing, silver, flute, apricot* and *hyacinth.*

Sounds like the makings of a nice day Down Under.

FAMOUS LAST WORDS

"I don't feel good."

I ran into a friend in a bookstore the other day and was astonished to see that she turned to the last page of every book she picked up and read the ending. When I questioned her about this curious practice she confessed that she always read the end of a book before deciding whether to buy it.

Since not knowing how things are going to come out is one of the main reasons for living, I can't imagine what perverse advantage this woman gains by finding out how something comes out before deciding to experience it.

I would no more want to know how a book turns out without reading it through than I would want to know in advance who won a tennis match or a football game. Granted, the precognition of sports events would quickly make one rich, if one enjoyed betting on a sure thing, but I would never give up suspense for mere money.

It is therefore only because I have already read the books involved, or don't intend to, that I am rather a collector of the last lines of novels, and so I am gratified to learn that this weakness also afflicts Devery Freeman, who was writing for *Punch* and *The New Yorker* when I was still writing for Miss Marien Keyes at Belmont High School.

Freeman recently sent me a piece called "Book Ends," which he wrote for *Punch* in 1935. "I can now thumb my nose at the short-sighted tutors who kept me in prep school for twelve years," it began, "and point to my scholarly work as a critic and fancier of last sentences of novels."

He went on to say that he got the idea when he skipped to the last page of Knut Hamsun's *August,* thus saving himself a lot of drudgery, and found that it ended as follows: "Some little planets dry up. Some little children die. . . . Then a fresh rumour of herring up at Eidsfjord."

Among the others Freeman found worthy of collecting were the last words of Stephen Crane's *Red Badge of Courage*: "Over the river a golden ray of sun came through the hosts of leaden rainclouds."

He classified this type as the Optimistic Weather Report, as opposed to the Pessimistic Weather Report exemplified by the last words of Romain Rolland's *Jean Christophe*: "Rain fell. Night fell."

That might also be placed in the Things Falling category, he pointed out, along with the last line of Arnold Bennett's *Lord Raingo*: "His jaw fell."

Freeman was also fond of the Blessed Event ending, typified by Ligget Reynolds in *Sweet and Low*: " 'Oliver,' she shouted, 'we're going to have a child.' "

The Blessed Event ending is somewhat clouded by uncertainty, he noted, in the last lines of Le Sage's *Gil Blas*: "Heaven has designed to send me two smiling babes . . . and if ever husband might venture so bold an hypothesis, I devoutly believe myself their father."

Since I never look at the endings of books I haven't finished, I didn't know that Dostoevski's *Brothers Karamazov* ends as follows: "Hurrah for Karamazov!"

Last lines in my own collection, some of which I actually quote from memory at cocktail parties, are chosen for any of several reasons—some because they are good, some because they are provocative, some because they are dreadful.

How does Winston Churchill end his six-volume memoir of World War II? "It only remains for me to express to the British people, for whom I have acted in these perilous years, my profound gratitude for the unflinching, unswerving support which they have given me during my task, and for the many expressions of kindness which they have shown toward their servant."

Ernest Hemingway's last lines are sometimes exquisite distillations of his style and theme. On the last page of *The Sun Also Rises*, the girl Brett, pressing close to the disenchanted Jake, says, "Oh, Jake, we could have had such a damned good time together." Jake ends it. "Yes . . . isn't it pretty to think so?" It was the last word of the lost generation.

And the last line of *A Farewell to Arms* is the essence of Hemingway: "After a while I went out and left the hospital and walked back to the hotel in the rain."

Almost as well known, and also definitive of its author, is the last line of F. Scott Fitzgerald's *The Great Gatsby*: "So we beat on, boats against the current, borne back ceaselessly into the past."

But enough of disenchantment and despair. I prefer to read books that end like Lauri Colwin's *Happy All the Time*, a contemporary novel about two likable young couples who have a lot of fun without succumbing to any of our era's popular hang-ups or kinky diversions. It ends: "They raised their glasses and, by the light of the candles, they drank to a truly wonderful life."

I don't know whether novelists work as hard on their last lines as they do on their first lines. I doubt that many novelists have been able to dash off that first line and first paragraph without grinding out a great many rejects. Every writer's wastebasket has been filled with the balled-up failures of his beginnings.

Oddly, I have had no trouble with either the first or final line of my own first novel, *Summer's End*. It begins: "It was the end of summer." It ends: "It only hurt when he laughed."

All I have to do is write the three hundred pages in between.

Have you ever studied the last lines of dying people?" asks Dan B. Genung, pastor of Mount Hollywood Congregational Church.

In a recent church newsletter, Genung says, he read of the death of a friend, Art Button, who tried feebly to explain to his pastor that he had four insurance plans he hoped would cover all expenses. "Then, his voice having failed, he got a pencil and wrote, 'God's plan is best.' "

I'm not sure I believe that story. A man whose life was ebbing away would not be able to write, would he? And anyway it sounds like a very poor legal arrangement to make at the end.

Genung says he takes great delight in the dying words of Samuel Upham, dean of Drew Theological Seminary, who evidently heard bedside friends conjecturing whether he had passed: "Is he dead yet?" one said, and a second suggested, "Feel his feet. Nobody ever died with warm feet." Upon which the patient said, "Joan of Arc did."

I like a man who can jest in the throes of death, but somehow I don't believe that story, either. Unfortunately, the departed have no remedy for misquotations of their final statements.

Genung recalls the supposed last words of one of my favorite people in history, the English writer Lady Mary Montagu, whom he accurately describes as "a woman of great courage and scandalous personal life." Her last words: "It's all been very interesting." I believe it.

Genung also reports that the last words of Edwin Markham, the poet, were: "Turn my face to see the sunrise." Like the famous last words of so many other poets, kings and philosophers, those seem a bit too suitable to me. I am skeptical of last words that are so lucid and concise and put their author in such a favorable light for posterity. I have an idea that most famous last words were actually next to last words, or have been edited by their auditors as a final favor to a departing friend, or invented out of whole cloth, for that matter.

It is interesting that Napoleon's last words were simply *"Tête d'armée,"* meaning "Head of the army." As Mark Twain pointed out in an essay on last words, Napoleon's were hardly appropriate to the ending of so grand a career. Twain argued that a person should never leave anything as important as his last words to the last hour of his life, when he is not likely to be in tip-top shape, and that he ought to write them out on a slip of paper, well in advance of the need, and even consult with friends, perhaps, on their merit.

He suggested that Napoleon's nephew, Emperor Louis Napoleon (who was then alive), might pay his respects to his uncle in his own last words, and at the same time make a graceful exit for himself by saying, "I am content to follow my uncle—still I do not wish to improve upon his last words. Put me down for *'Tête d'armée.'"*

Surely the most ironic of last words were those of Daniel Webster: "I still live!" These three words have come ringing down to us as a testament to the man's indomitable spirit. But I am more inclined to believe the story that his nurse had been instructed to give him a spoonful of brandy every half hour while he lived, and "when the clock chimed and the brandy was not immediately produced, the great man opened his mouth and uttered his last words as a reminder."

From the supposed last words that I have received from readers, I have determined that there are three kinds: those I believe, those I don't believe, and those I don't believe but would like to believe.

Those I believe, alas, are rarely poetic or illuminating, or even a neat summation of their author's life and philosophy. They are rather the sort of things we would expect a person to say as he took leave of his wits, along with everything else. Rex Nath recalls, for example, that Luther Burbank, father of the Burbank potato, dying at seventy-seven, said, "I don't feel good."

I believe it; but I would not believe it if some bedside Bowdler had changed it to "I don't feel well."

From Lois Markwith, archivist of *The Los Angeles Times*, I learn that its founder, General Harrison Gray Otis, was having breakfast in bed and, recognizing "a rupture of the heart as fatal," according to a contemporary account, said in a low, unexcited tone, "I am gone," and died. Franklin D. Roosevelt said, "I have a terrific headache."

There should be a special category for those that are believable because they were spoken immediately before an unexpected seizure, while the author was supposedly in fine fettle. Ed Shoaff, the La Canada encyclopedist of quotations, sends a clipping from *Reader's Digest* recalling that Alben Barkley, perhaps the happiest of our vice-presidents, was making a speech at Washington and Lee University, in Virginia, and fell dead on the stage immediately after saying, "I would rather be a servant in the House of the Lord than sit in the seat of the mighty."

That seems too good to be true, but the contemporary newspaper accounts are agreed on it. I prefer the remark attributed to his wife when someone tried to console her by saying, "Now he's in heaven." Mrs. Barkley said, "No, he'd still be at the gate telling St. Peter a story."

Bing Crosby's supposed last words, as quoted by the press, sound probable enough. Walking from the eighteenth green with his foursome, he said, "That was a great game, fellers," and fell dead.

Ben Irwin recalls a gentleman, alas anonymous, who was asked by his wife, rather callously, "Do you want to be buried or cremated?" and he said, "Surprise me, love." Now that's panache.

(That story has been authoritatively elucidated by Robert A. Schiller, as follows: "You're right. That was panache. And that husband, from this date forward need no longer be 'alas anonymous.' It was my father, Roland Schiller, who said it to my mother some years ago. And the exact quote was a simple 'Surprise me.' No 'love.' A more fitting retort to a callous question. Brevity being the soul of wit, I submit that the answer, sans 'love,' is wittier and as brief as you can get. My mother is gone these many years, God having apparently punished her for that callous question; but my father is still tossing off one-liners at the ripe old age of ninety-one. He surprises everyone.")

Helen Chrostowski recalls that Gertrude Stein's last conversation was recorded by Duncan Sutherland. "Just before she died she asked, 'What is the answer?' No answer came. She laughed and said, 'In that case, what is the question?'" You know Gertrude. It's probably true.

Floyd A. Moos of Northridge writes that he begins a classroom review of the basic rules of grammar every semester with the following quote: "These are the dying words of Dominique Bouhours (1628–1702): 'I am about to—or I am going to—die; either expression is used.'

"After a dramatic pause, I admonish my class that if D. Bouhours could spend precious dying moments concerned with language usage, the least the students could do is spend five minutes proofreading their essays."

I applaud Professor Moos for his admirable intentions, but I wonder whether any of his students have quibbled over his illustration. "I am about to die" would indeed have applied precisely to M. Bouhours's own situation; but "I am going to die" would have applied to everyone, since we are all going to die, and thus was not an apt alternative for a man who took care to achieve precision in language.

I have always hoped that my own last words would be, "Heigh ho—is there any more champagne?" Mark Nichols sends the heartening news that I am in good company. "Your proposed final words," he writes, "are derivative of Anton Chekhov's, who said, before expiring, at forty-four: 'It's been a long time since I had champagne.'" (And Jan Paderewski, asked if he would like champagne, politely answered, "Please.")

William Saroyan, the exuberant Armenian who died recently in Fresno, seems to have taken Mark Twain's advice and written his last words ahead of time. "Five days before his death ," writes George Masonian, of Fresno, "he called the Associated Press to make this final statement for publication after his death: 'Everybody has got to die, but I have always believed an exception would be made in my case. Now what?'"

My guess is that, like Gertrude, he got no answer.

If I get my champagne, I hope I still have grace enough, at the very end, to give my loved ones a final imperative:

"Have a nice day!"